SATURN

FATAL ATTRACTION

ADAM SMITH

Winchester, UK
Washington, USA)

First published by O Books, 2007
O Books is an imprint of John Hunt Publishing Ltd.,
The Bothy, Deershot Lodge, Park Lane, Ropley, Hants, SO24 0BE, UK
office1@o-books.net
www.o-books.net

Distribution in:

UK and Europe
Orca Book Services
orders@orcabookservices.co.uk
Tel: 01202 665432 Fax: 01202 666219 Int. code (44)

USA and Canada
NBN
custserv@nbnbooks.com
Tel: 1 800 462 6420 Fax: 1 800 338 4550

Australia and New Zealand
Brumby Books
sales@brumbybooks.com.au
Tel: 61 3 9761 5535 Fax: 61 3 9761 7095

Far East (offices in Singapore, Thailand, Hong Kong, Taiwan)
Pansing Distribution Pte Ltd
kemal@pansing.com
Tel: 65 6319 9939 Fax: 65 6462 5761

South Africa
Alternative Books
altbook@peterhyde.co.za
Tel: 021 447 5300 Fax: 021 447 1430

Text copyright Adam Smith 2007

Design: Stuart Davies

ISBN-13: 978 1 905047 86 4
ISBN-10: 1 905047 86 X

A CIP catalogue record for this book is available from the British Library.

Printed in the US by Maple Vail

SATURN

FATAL ATTRACTION

ADAM SMITH

BOOKS

Winchester, UK
Washington, USA

CONTENTS

PREFACE   vii

THE CELESTIAL ANTI-HERO
The Defining Influence   1

THE DEVIL YOU KNOW
Maya and the Myth of Saturn   14

MATURE REFLECTION
Saturn's sign and the Inner Adult.   26

CROSSROADS BLUES
Saturn transiting the planets   45

WHAT'S YOUR PROBLEM?
Saturn Transiting the Houses   85

FATAL ATTRACTION
Karmic Connections   142

ARE YOU EXPERIENCED?
Astrologers, Fate and Saturn Strategies. 156

APPENDIX ONE
Astrology down the line   174

APPENDIX 2
ZODIACAL HOUSES.   179

NOTES   184

'Unlimited possibilities are not suited to man; if they existed, his life would only dissolve in the boundless. To become strong, a man's life needs the limitations ordained by duty and voluntarily accepted. The individual attains significance as a free spirit only by surrounding himself with these limitations and by determining for himself what his duty is'.

I Ching, Hexagram 60 'Limitation' (Wilhelm edition).

PREFACE

In the same way as biographies of famous people are rewritten every few years in the light of fresh research, new events in the lives of planets come to light every day. The more notorious the character, the more stories that grow up around them and most astrologers have their tales to tell of Saturn. It is in the nature of this shadowy body to create action, adjustment and 'interesting times', which in turn produces more material worth writing about. Bad news makes a good story, so rather than give way to a daringly novel or completely revisionist stance I seem to have focused quite heavily on Saturn's debit side in this book. Pretending that he is never tough is no good: tough is what Saturn does and he would not be nearly so compelling otherwise.

There is a fair amount of abstract material and metaphysical speculation here too, but Saturn is a planet that inclines anyone to take refuge in philosophy. My own views are coloured by an Eastern-oriented outlook, which takes karma and reincarnation as given. Any reader uncomfortable with this perspective can interpret the book in the light of whatever philosophic system they prefer. The occasional references to the Chinese *I Ching* are self-explanatory in context, while the Vedic astrology need not confuse a Western astrologer, because the two interpretations of Saturn are virtually identical. The only difference is that, if anything, Vedic authorities take an even dimmer view of 'Sani' than we do. My real intention is to reflect the nature of the planet itself and show how Saturn really works in a nitty-gritty way, especially by transit. The real-world examples of Saturn at work stand on their own and hopefully speak more eloquently for themselves than any amount of abstract theorising.

Astrologers inevitably bring their own issues to the table and the perceptive reader may surmise that I have a somewhat over-bearing Saturn in my own chart. True. I also began writing this book under successive hard knocks to my natal Sun, Moon and Ascendant, by the end of which time, I felt fairly besieged. Had I completed the whole book during this difficult period, its tone would have been much less charitable, so for once I can feel grateful to Saturn for making me take my time. There are no delineations of *natal* Saturn by aspect or through the houses, though information on these can be inferred from the chapters on transits. Rather than attempt a definitive account, it is probably better that any astrologer simply adds his or her own voice to the discussion.

A big thank you to everyone who helped me in the writing of this book, in particular, Adam Fronteras, Enid Williams and Jessica Adams.

CHAPTER ONE

THE CELESTIAL ANTI-HERO.

The Defining Influence

We try to be modern and constructive in our astrology these days, but for most people, Saturn is the Bogeyman, if not the very Devil. An enlightened critical reappraisal in recent years has emphasised his sturdy, practical qualities, but Saturn's murky character is still one of the first things the student in astrology learns. We come up with an uncomfortable bump against the curious word 'malefic' and discover that Saturn is the very embodiment of the term. Growth, grounding and spiritual wisdom are part of the picture, but this seems only another way of saying Saturn makes us sadder but wiser. Work, boundaries, ageing and fear: no matter how we try to spin it, all the weary jokes and stories told about what a drag life is centre round the Ringed Planet and his disagreeable issues. His reputation cannot on the whole be considered a conspiracy.

Saying that he can be tough and bring unpleasant experiences, however, is simply to recognise that Saturn is a factor that jerks us all out of our comfort zone and forces us to grow up. His impact is deeply resented because he requires hard work and action, and most of us are better at talking than actually doing. Grasping the nettle and getting Saturn onside is something few people completely master, for it is in his nature never to let us entirely relax and feel that we have arrived. He makes us mature and disillusioned, but his constant vigilance and challenging influence equally never allow us to become jaded or blasé. We become authorities through Saturn's placement, savants and connoisseurs, and not dabblers or dilettantes. By accepting his challenge and becoming good at it, there is cause for ultimate optimism and we are given the opportunity to show a little class.

Astrology is specifically concerned with fate and timing in most people's eyes and Saturn is the ruler of these dimensions within the art itself. Mercury is the *traditional* planetary ruler of astrology, in his capacity as Messenger of the Gods, while Uranus, the Sky God, has come to represent astrology in the modern sense of it being a maverick profession[1]. But even if we defer to its 'official' rulers, there is still a case for saying Saturn is astrology's defining planet, the one factor above all that it pays to know about. He brings astrologers most of their clients and is implicated in much of our meatiest astrology. The best stories and case histories in the average stargazer's files have more instances of Saturn at work than probably any other planet. The measurement of time is also that which distinguishes astrology from other divinatory practices: Tarot, Runes, *I Ching,* or scrying. In craft parlance, *radical* means 'fit to judge', and says that something is active in the horoscope, or changes are decisively happening. There is *movement.* Saturn, by transit at least, seems always radical, never slight or inconsequential, for we are all too well aware of his placement at any given time. The heavenly body with the beautiful rings symbolically represents boundaries and limitations, and this instantly identifiable image practically qualifies as the logo of astrology.

For millennia, Saturn was the outermost planet in our solar

system, the furthest planet visible to the naked eye, and still he marks the threshold before the generational Uranus, Neptune and Pluto - and whatever now lies beyond. Perhaps the modern world needed dedicated symbols for the new phenomena of the Internet, communism, nuclear power and so on, but until recently, the outer bodies were happily redundant. Practically speaking, they did not even exist. It is not so easy to imagine a universe without Saturn. The point is fanciful, but while Uranus, Neptune and Pluto are so often seen as the most calamitous and awe inspiring astrological agents in the cosmos, there is another planet who has been around for a while longer, who carries a good deal of weight. No doubt the 'invisible' outer trio make their presence felt, but they seem to belong to a different order of creation. They cannot truly compete with Saturn's decisive influence, his overbearing power and sheer physicality. In the search for yet more symbols, more knowledge and revelation, it is easy for astrologers to overlook the potential of the model they already have.

Saturn therefore represents the symbolic point where the tangible world begins. Beyond him, the astrological universe dissolves into finer, psychic territory and infinitely distant and slow moving specks that signify the group consciousness. Saturn's frontier position is the symbol of the relative world itself, the outer shadow that defines the light and the bottom line of material existence. His slow moving nature and cold, dry quality brings crystallisation, where the image is of an object taking solid form through being frozen or moulded. The concept of light is meaningless without the dark and Saturn's shadow is that which defines a thing. Anything infinite is *un*-manifest, and Saturn represents both limitation and the resulting physical materialisation. From a relative point of view, we understand the world and each other in terms of that which we are *not*, as much as what we are, and this is expressed by Saturn's status as the ultimate ruler of literal, physical matter. An object must be one thing or the other, not both.

Saturn also rules structure in the human body, the skeleton and the bare bones. His defining shadow throws into sharp relief whatever he touches and the best way to truly appreciate a given astrological point, be it ever so obscure, is to have Saturn transit it. Whether it is a personal planet, a sign, house, asteroid, hypothetical point, *anything*, Saturn coming into contact with it, especially by conjunction shows its fundamental nature. There are some vague and apparently tenuous associations in astrology: try defining the qualities of the Twelfth house, for example, to a non-initiate and reconciling how the zodiacal area of libraries and hospitals ties in with past lives, large pets and hidden enemies[2]. However, Saturn will transit through our Twelfth house at some point, and all of these disparate and apparently ill-defined elements come home and achieve an almost miraculous sense of solidity and reality. After Saturn's transit we understand the thing in our bones. We just *know* it.

In the relative, dark-light Saturnian world, every attribute also contains the seed of its opposite. We build up structures wherever Saturn is found, but these structures must continue to grow, and not become empty vessels with no practical purpose. Traditions, organisations, relationships and institutions continue for as long as their guiding spirit and real-world effectiveness remains, but once this is lost, the purely material side eventually withers and dies. In one of his many paradoxical aspects, transiting Saturn shows us where to limit the material itself and where inner worth should take over. We do not always do well at this in the West, but Saturn shows the occasional need for discipline, austerity and self-denial. This is entailed in his traditional rulership of monks and renunciants, along with, for example, his association with The Hermit card in the Tarot. Much of the related tension and pain of Saturn revolves around the resistance between structure and austerity: it is one thing to renounce the world, but questions arise if we find the Saturnian world has renounced *us*.

Chronology is a Saturn word, of course, describing linear, sequential time, which is also the most valuable commodity in the universe. Time is simply a necessary consequence of the relative sphere, where events do not all happen simultaneously, in the eternal, spiritual present. Hand in hand with time is gravity, the other essentially Saturnian power that came into being at the very instant of creation, keeping the planets moving in their orbits and making the temporal world conform to set, predictable patterns. This has significance for astrologers of course, but is good news for anyone wishing to keep solid ground under their feet and the sky from falling on their head. Some kind of consistency is always welcome in practical terms, though kept up indefinitely becomes a dreary sameness where nothing out of the ordinary ever happens and tomorrow is exactly the same as today. Time and gravity's downward push create wrinkles and the physical signs of ageing, and the same goes for the sense of a weighty mentality. Anyone said to possess *gravitas* as a personal quality is likely to have a prominent Saturn in their chart and a positive Saturnian role model is also said to be someone with 'weight'. 'Light', on the other hand, may mean illuminated or insubstantial, but either way is the very opposite of both Saturnian darkness and heaviness.

On the birth chart, Saturn-as-shadow has come to represent the darker side of the psyche. There is a danger of treating all such psychological models as Holy Scripture, but the Jungian shadow is a perfect metaphor for unconscious and destructive human behaviour. The shadow is essentially ignorance, which obscures the consequences of our own negative actions, and where we behave from base, negative motives. This absence of knowing is the root of all evil and suffering. Saturn is only the shadow at his most primitive level of course, but even at best he leads us to act in a compromised and conservative way. What we have, we hold, and rather than stretch ourselves or experiment, Saturn cautions us to stay where we are and settle for the Devil we know.

This kind of response is essentially rooted in fear – fear of losing the self by stepping outside of the strict Saturnian confines. Outside is the unknown, the Void, which at its ultimate level is represented by death, which is of course another Saturnian illusion, albeit a persuasive one. There is no pre-existent road that leads out of the dark country of Saturn; we have to create it ourselves. By working and facing up to his challenges, it is as if we lay down stepping stones that lead across a river and out of the darkness. Otherwise, the confinement of Saturn becomes comfortingly familiar, and by refusing to look outside we follow the pattern of the recidivist who always finds ways of getting re-arrested because prison is all that he knows. Breaking out of Saturn's captivity, in the form of his natal placement and difficult aspects, takes courage, perseverance and a sense of faith that there is more to life outside of our own lights and limitations.

Saturnian diversity on a birth chart also emphasises the idea of separateness, especially when challengingly aspected. The resistance that he represents at its most basic level[3] becomes a resistance to any kind of strong spontaneous feeling that cannot be materially reckoned with. His cold, dry, slow-moving nature does not easily allow anything to *flow*. Emotions are slippery and intangible and a stressful natal Saturn's approach is often *over-literal* in matters of the heart. Saturn understands things to be material and discrete, and the idea that subtle sensations can be both one thing and the other, or neither one nor the other, is the thing of his nightmares. Saturn is not spontaneous or intuitive, but rather fears the writing between the lines, viewing emotion as a rather insidious impulse that brings the tangible world crashing down.

Despite this lack of emotional subtlety, the strongly Saturnian individual can show surprising reserves of empathy and compassion, based precisely on their own tough experiences. This person is also admirably practical and rather than providing mere tea and sympathy, he is more concerned with steps that actively alleviate suffering. Saturn's home sign of Capricorn famously embodies his recognisable qualities: ambition, prudence, pragmatism, and the more familiar saturnine temperament: dry, understated, pessimistic, melancholic. But a little emphasised point is that Capricorn's symbol, the Goat, and also its glyph, have fish's tails: it is in fact a *Water* Goat, implying the sign's latent emotional side. Planets placed in Capricorn tend to bury this feeling quality at the expense of the more characteristic worldly ambition. Any planet aspected strongly by Saturn also hides reserves of priceless world-weary humour. Irony is a response to the disappointments of life; the recognition that if you didn't laugh, you would probably cry.

Saturn's rulership of both Capricorn and Aquarius shows his both his traditional face and also his more modern and progressive side. Aquarius is more familiarly known as an idealistic, rebellious Uranus-ruled sign, but Saturn-Chronos was a revolutionary in his own time, too. He rebelled against his father Uranus to prevent him beating up on his mother, Gaia. It is more in the Aquarian character to shock and get a reaction, but this may be through a reaction*ary*, deeply conservative attitude that gets a perverse kick from taking the opposing view of whatever is the current trend or received wisdom. Planets in Aquarius believe rules are made to be broken, but not if they created the rules. Everyone can think what they like, as long as they think the same as the Aquarian. It is more accurate to see the Saturn-ruled side of Aquarius as representing what happens *after* The Revolution, once the old order has been torn down, the government overthrown and the once-radical ideals have become the new Saturnian orthodoxy.

Mercifully, alongside Saturn's rulership of walls and boundaries is contained the idea of doorways, passages and portals. The confines represented by Saturn's natal placement are not meant to be absolute and eternal, but restraining qualities that hold us in temporary check. The Lord of the Door represents not only the passage of time in a general sense, but his twenty-nine year orbit neatly encapsulates significant seven-year periods. Like the phases of the Moon[4], the applying and separating aspects of Saturn are fundamental building blocks of experience. It is truer to see Saturn's orbit not as a circle, but a spiral, which gives a better understanding of a time-centred, four dimensional dynamic. The limitations represented by Saturn can be crossed or surmounted at

certain times in life, at precise ages, or ag.
metaphysical breakthrough has been achieved
rarefied, but most often amounts merely t(
absorbing the lesson that Saturn represents on th
refusing to run away from it. It is that simple an   ground.
Whether we look at Saturn and see a wall, or a portal, says a great
deal about us as individuals.

To the extent to which natal Saturn is stressfully placed or
aspected, his confines appear permanent and inevitable and to a
greater or lesser extent we submit to them. This may be through
either a sign of a quiescent, fatalistic attitude, or a dignified
knowledge of our own self-worth. But Saturn's limitations are
themselves limited - once again, they are *temporary* restrictions
that take us down certain avenues until they are gradually eroded
by the magic formula of courage and hard work. There appears to
be no mystical key to The Lord of The Door other than effort,
and his various challenges are things lived through rather than
instantly resolved. No matter how it sometimes seems, though,
Saturn is demanding, but not vindictive and as well as exacting
obedience, he also confers eventual rewards. Saturn *delivers*, both
in the sense of producing the goods and also of setting us free.

The manifest world gives us height, breadth, depth, and time,
but also fate, which is a fifth Saturnian dimension. As human men
and women, most of us are basically lazy, and given the choice,
prefer to put our feet up, daydream and take the easy option every
time. The lessons and insights that come from his struggle are what
is said to make Saturn worthwhile, but many of us would prefer no
insight and no struggle. We also lack the scope or imagination to
appreciate what is truly best for us at all times, which is where

n, in his capacity as the Karmic Lord enters in. We may be well behaved, look after our health and always do the very best we can, but fate and karma are the intangible, mysterious qualities over which we have very little apparent control. This is a fairly scary refection in itself. The intimidating, atavistic quality of fate and the element of sheer egotism in us, means we do not readily accept anything that has not been realised by our own hand.

Yet without Saturn's firm pushes and equally firm limitations, we would be content to do nothing we do not have to and our evolutionary growth would slow down, stop, and eventually start sliding backwards. An obnoxious event or impulse enters into our world, for which we have by no means volunteered, and gives us a far more testing examination than we thought necessary. It is generally only after the event, perhaps quite a while afterwards, that the lessons are grudgingly accepted as useful and constructive. This is Saturn in his parental image: a strict, stern, patriarchal figure whom we may respect, but find it harder to love. This aspect of Saturn also provides some clue to his exaltation in Libra: the planet of karma seems naturally at home in a sign whose emblem is the Scales. There is also the sense of finding a middle way between laziness and excessive effort; fear and controlling overcompensation.

While Saturn rules fate, however, he cannot be called fickle. Anything but. As spirits inside human bodies, our mission is to learn how to deal with and manipulate the basic building blocks of matter and work in the material world is like stone masonry, chipping away one stroke at a time. Physically shifting matter is one aspect of Saturnian work, but even on a psychic level, Saturn symbolises dead thoughts, negative, stuck thinking and an obstacle that must be removed or overcome. On an esoteric level, these old thought patterns become crystallised and encrusted over lifetimes, and are the very thing that bring about continual rebirth and incarnation. Habits, past mistakes and unfulfilled desires steadily accrue and the natal placement of Saturn represents the most compelling lesson we have to learn in relation to our karmic past.

For Saturn's rulership of karma is hard to reconcile without necessarily accepting reincarnation. The phrase 'karmic astrology' is a tautology - one might as well say 'stellar astrology'. If we accept one thing in the chart is karmic, it all is, though points like Saturn and on a different level, the Nodes and the Twelfth house, do seem to have a specific connection with lessons taken over from past lives. Pointing the finger at Saturn for our misadventures is somewhat wide of the mark in any case. The Lord of Karma has no intrinsic malevolence, but he is simply the most obvious carrier of fate and destiny. The lessons learned through his natal placement and transits are the results of our own actions and *blaming* Saturn is simply shooting the messenger.

Saturn's positive qualities of dignity, work, worldly wisdom, leadership, are all forms of triumph over adversity. There is a lasting physical monument and he wants to leave a statement behind, a legacy. He bestows enterprise or leadership ability, and if not the subtlest interpersonal skills, then a certain base cunning. The coarsening effect of Saturn by transit makes us ultimately pragmatic, if not a little cynical, but the strong Saturn type is canny and persevering, with a latent executive streak that knows how to get things done. Success is usually cited as a combination of hard work, timing and fate (or good karma) so Saturn has a decisive influence here, too. He *is* the planet of success. His lessons come through effort, stoicism and acceptance and the eventual reward is enhanced freedom and maturity. Nobody knows better than the Saturnian character that it is lonely at the top, but he prefers to take this burden upon himself if it means having a position that cannot be taken away.

Looked at from this perspective, it is fair to say Saturn, more than any other, is the planet of *potential* – he sometimes does not appear to have much positive credit or goodwill except to the extent that we work on his issues. The clock has to be physically wound up before it starts ticking and the earth has to be dug up before anything will grow in it. These are Saturn truths. Whatever we get from Saturn, we have to earn and even when strong and well-aspected, he simply signifies a capacity and *acceptance* of more work. This seems a pretty understated beneficence, but in fact it is an enormous advantage on planet Earth, for anyone not afraid of hard work can do almost anything they set their mind to. Without effort, Saturn's influence is to provide purely 'negative benefits' – shielding a man from his fears and limitations, until the Lord of Karma decides the time and circumstance when he is ready to face up to them. Once again, it is often not for many years that we realise that a desire apparently *withheld* from us can be a good thing.

If 'potential' seems like faint praise, then few if any of the other planets contain as much potential as Saturn. Jupiter is the good news in astrology, the Greater Benefic where we achieve a good outcome through spontaneous positive mental programming: we expect the best, which creates positive conditions for success. His effects are often subtle, but generally pleasing. Saturn, however, is a planet that truly contains the promise of becoming what we make of it, and where any effort is rewarded with results that are, if not permanent, then substantive and long lasting. It is like being paid in gold bars, or blue-chip shares that mature wonderfully and pay off for the long term. Winning with Saturn also means we have made it on our own terms and do not owe our success to anyone else. Jupiter's effects feel like unbidden gifts, whereas Saturn's rewards are frequently hard earned. Jupiter is the heir and Saturn is the self-made man[5].

So the understanding that Saturn is the surly sentinel that *prevents* us doing anything we want to do means he has been seriously miscast. The Task Master can be viewed less as a slave driver cracking the whip over us human galley slaves, but more a kind of grand ringmaster or impresario. Saturn is like a pushy parent, or ambitious agent-manager, twirling his moustache and plotting and scheming on our behalf. We must not disappoint him and cannot rest up, for he has big plans, and if we co-operate, a grand destiny for us to fulfil. He is not a villain or tyrant, but an anti-hero; uncharismatic and frequently misunderstood, who in his mysterious way only desires the very best for us. Any dystopian view of him must also be seen in the context that he is only one planet. *One* factor in astrology where the message is to work hard and get it right is not much in the overall scheme, however important he is, and by painting Saturn in such dramatic, uncompromising terms, perhaps we are only giving The Old Devil his due.

CHAPTER TWO

THE DEVIL YOU KNOW
Maya and the Myth of Saturn

Saturn's natal position makes everything very serious. There appears to be *a great deal at stake* wherever he is placed, so we tread carefully through the webs and the issues of Saturn's sign and house signify a pursuit of excellence and a fundamental statement of who we are. A man may hold cripplingly high standards, refusing to accept anything less than the very best, though the best often only comes with time and practice. It is not enough to muddle through with Saturn, but it is as if we expect to make some truly profound and meaningful statement through his placement. This is very well, if the effort is actually applied, but all too often the burden of extra work and responsibility means the road is never embarked upon.

Looking from the outside at other people's Saturn position, it often appears they are making life unnecessarily hard for themselves. *Why does* the person with Saturn in the Tenth house make such heavy weather of their career, deliberating endlessly over different options and not simply getting a job and moving on? Likewise, the talented person with Saturn in the Fifth house desperately wants to express himself artistically, but cannot simply get on with it unless there is a stone-cold prior guarantee that he will be the next Mozart or Michelangelo. The same applies to every sign and house position of Saturn, as we endlessly analyse and agonise, desperate not to put a foot wrong. What's going on?

Western astrology takes its symbolic cues from ancient Greece and Rome, but the motifs of Saturn have parallels in myths from all over the world. For example, Saturn has a great deal in common with the Yogic concept of *Maya*. Maya is the interplay of the whole material world, which at the most exalted spiritual level is realised as illusory. Buddhists may recognize this as pure Mind; an objectified cosmic dream, which ultimately is only dispelled by reaching Enlightenment. Perhaps it is unfair to saddle any one planet with this burden, but Saturn is the ruler of base materialism and the temporal world. This is consistent with the portrayal of Maya as the trickster who ensnares us in his web and the personalised Biblical representation of the Devil himself. Eastern philosophy says that the appearance of Maya is due to ignorance, which is in turn the ultimate cause of suffering. The level of understanding at which we perceive Maya determines the extent to which it is real. So at last, the world is pure ideal, but few of us live from day to day at this supreme level of consciousness.

Saturn, in either his natal or transiting position brings us up against apparent obstacles and frustration, but like the experience of Maya, these boundaries are in fact only provisional. We give Saturn's shadowy limitations greater substance to the extent that we identify and run away from them. The restrictions of fate and time are relative, and by working positively and facing the challenges, a man eventually makes himself free of Saturn's bonds. A stressfully aspected natal Saturn is one that cannot operate without a certain amount of adjustment, which makes effort more intimidating, and results take longer to achieve. But working at Saturn in any condition is never time wasted. Ensnaring ourselves in a tangled, tenuous world on the other hand, around the refusal to recognise the consequences of our own behaviour, is the worst possible approach, as is illustrated by the myth of Saturn-Chronos.

Chronos

To recap: The Greek Saturn, Chronos, took his mother Gaia's part against his tyrannical father, Uranus, the Sky God. Using the sickle given to him by Gaia, Chronos castrated his father and usurped his title King of the Gods. Chronos then held supreme power, though with his head lying uneasily for constant fear that someone would in turn overthrow him. He proceeded to eat all of his children to prevent a celestial palace coup, which did not endear him to his wife Rhea, who hid their son Jupiter until he was strong enough to stand up to the old man. Young Jupiter then brought his father's fears crashing back to him by seizing power, banishing Chronos to the earth and establishing himself as the Olympian King.

A good story, but what does it all mean? There are many interpretations, among which the idea of the 'Sins of the Father' is instructive. Saturn hated his father and rebelled against him, yet he re-enacted the same pattern with his own children, with the same disastrous consequences. Whether it is a strictly fated occurrence, or a product of environment and conditioning, how often do people fall into exactly the parenthood traps that they vowed never to repeat? Or, like Chronos, they feared their own parents and feel it incumbent to ensure that their own children are frightened of them. On a more esoteric level, karma is in fact handed down through bloodlines. When a father dies, the unresolved karma from his last lifetime is passed on to the next available material vessel, his children.

The myth also says something about Saturnian ambition and his willingness to take responsibility: Chronos decided that something needed to be done about Uranus and at the same time, saw an opportunity to make something of himself. This is characteristic Saturn-influenced behaviour. Saturn defines himself in terms of status or standing, and will go to great lengths to accomplish his goals. It does not always mean taking such large risks as Chronos, but opportunism is a big motivation. Once a man has arrived in a position of authority, he may become a beneficent boss, or an overbearing despot. Either he helps others get along, or pulls the ladder of opportunity up after him, for fear of being emulated or overtaken. The wise Saturnian chief realises the karmic consequences of his actions and that by helping others he helps himself. As the *I Ching* says, 'To rule truly is to serve'.

Chronos's attitude towards his children also illustrates the Saturnian propensity to hate or reject the things that we have created. People also hate the things that they fear, so Saturn frequently represents a fear of creativity or self-expression. We wish for a lasting legacy through our Saturnian effort, but the struggle to give birth to an idea, career, or any attainment at all has been so difficult that we have little subsequent love for it. Likewise, once Saturn has transited a natal house, we are heartily sick of its mundane affairs for a long time afterwards.

Most of all, though, the myth of Chronos depicts Saturn's capacity for projection through fear. Saturn toppled his own father, which means someone will topple him and at some guilty, half-conscious level he knows it. He tries to avoid his fate by controlling his environment, and becomes a tyrant in the same way as his father. If he had been a more modern parent and perhaps talked to his children instead of eating them, Chronos may have remained King, but perhaps even Gods have their high-level karma to live out. Fear manifests itself, and the steps Chronos took to avoid his fears only set up the inevitability of them coming about. Psychologically speaking, it is common to see Saturnian problems on the birth-chart mirroring the mythic Chronos and stemming from negative projections about the world that become cruel self-fulfilling prophecies. This is classic Saturn in his archetype as the Devil or trickster. The stratagems and mechanisms used to *avoid* the perceived pain and problems of Saturn, as represented by his sign, house and aspect, appear to be the very things that bring them about. Avoidance of Saturn, or of fate if we prefer, eventually leads to a degree of overcompensation, and here we are caught in the very behaviour we are most afraid of. Saturn causes most hardship when acted upon, or *reacted to* out of fear, and while we may experience difficulties in any case, looking at Saturn as if through the gaps in our fingers virtually guarantees we bump into every possible obstacle. The image of fate is like being pursued by a speeding train: we can run away for a while, but it will surely catch up and it is much easier if we simply jump aboard. The changes will happen anyway.

To use a very simple example, people with Saturn in Pisces or perhaps the Twelfth house are said to be afraid of institutions and confinement. So they may refuse a doctor's appointment if there is the slightest fear they will have to go to hospital. This continues until it becomes absolutely imperative they be committed, where they end up spending far longer than if they had been checked out at the first sign of trouble. Or take the individual with Saturn in Aries who is frightened of asserting himself. He fears that nobody will like him, yet he manifests this fear and becomes unpopular by boorishly overcompensating for his natural reticence. There are numerous mundane examples of this Saturnian projection: people carry guns or knives for fear of meeting somebody else as paranoid as themselves. In political life, a government's defence budget is in direct proportion to the amount of fear prevalent in the world. Yet the more arms are created, the more the sum of global anxiety increases. There is a fine line between facing fear and the sense of hubris and reckless overcompensation that are its opposites.

Saturn's tale is set against the backdrop of his father and his children, but echoes of the myth are not restricted solely to family scenarios. People coming up the hard way in their career often achieve success through precisely the early privation and lack of emotional stroking signified by Saturn. 'Sweet are the uses of adversity' perhaps, except the fruits are often rather sour. A chip on the shoulder, perhaps in the form of a prominent square or opposition to a personal planet, provides the future Saturnian big shot's incentive for success. Using his discontent for positive motivation is very well, except the sense of perpetual grievance may remain even after he has 'made it'. Upon arrival in the Promised Land, the thrusting Saturnian type turns the tables on his former oppressors, which in his distorted reckoning includes almost everyone, by way of projecting his shadow outwards. Nobody is left in any doubt who is the new boss. If he becomes a truly tyrannical figure, he may set himself up for a fall after the fashion of Chronos, but this is of course Shadow-influenced behaviour at its very worst. Difficult natal aspects from Saturn need not manifest this fully-blown megalomaniac sense, but Saturn's myth merely provides a cautionary tale of behaviour to guard against.

There is a kind of reverse sympathy at work here – a fatal attraction or *un*sympathetic magic that determines that a man's unconscious, unwanted scenarios get played out despite himself. No matter how unfashionable or unpalatable, there is a suggestion that the experimentation undergone through Saturn's lessons cannot be *completely* avoided. We are all conditioned by karma to some extent. While confining him to the closet merely means that Saturn is expressed in a negligent or unwitting way, if Saturn signifies fated occurrences and work that *has* to be done, then there is nothing to be gained by trying to avoid the issues that he represents on the birth-chart. Boundaries and hard work are necessary elements to life too, and evasive manoeuvres usually mean the portal door swings back doubly hard on the rebound.

Yet it is not quite enough to deconstruct Saturn qualities as simple fearful psychic projections. Yes, the pitfalls and prejudices symbolized by natal Saturn are exaggerated in our own minds like distorted reflections in a hall of mirrors, but his boundaries arise from an innate metaphysical condition that seems real enough. Like the interplay of Maya, our limitations appear perfectly real on the level that we experience them. The paradox is that we are frightened of the apparent wall or precipice represented by Saturn, but until we work through or leap over, the restrictions continue to oppress. There is an objective element to the Saturnian fear and need for structure, limitations and boundaries, which is determined by our individual karma. This element is negotiable, however, and should be gradually eroded over time, which is of course Saturn's currency. It is in the nature of Saturn, be it through his sign, house or aspects, to get easier over time, or else we get better at handling him; or perhaps these are the same thing.

Fate manifesting through fear is encapsulated in the wonderful Celtic word, *weird*[6]. The Weird of Saturn comes from a karmic predisposition to be wary in a certain area of life, where there is a specific lesson to learn. A presentiment or foreknowledge often accompanies a fated situation, as we anticipate that something momentous is afoot. The classic fatal attraction is to something we sense is dangerous, but cannot resist. There may be an actual feeling of fascination or *déjà vu*, as we are stretched or tested beyond the limits of our imagination. We have a foreboding that a given situation does not feel right and we wish to avoid it. So we back off and back off, only to find we eventually come full circle and end up 'backing into' the thing we intended to evade. Avoiding 'A' in favour of 'B', we get 'A' anyway. The myth of Saturn embodies this idea, and Chronos himself must have felt something similar when confronted by his son Jupiter, wielding a sharp, pointy thunderbolt. Yet it is only when we look back that we appreciate that an experience had been *meant*, and there was no escaping it.

Time and experience bring a gradual change, where we can grow through necessary karmic lessons, of which Saturn is the most gross and obvious symbol. Where we are inwardly and consciousness-wise is where we are at in our lives. Our mind-level is raised by counselling, meditation and all manner of therapies, but the nature of Saturn is the basic template of life and there is little use trying to get ahead of the necessary sequence of events. The perspective that comes from Saturn making an aspect to itself, another planet, or when it moves through a house is organic and very hard or impossible to replace or replicate by any other means.

It is the difference between understanding a thing rationally and *knowing it* through direct experience. Many people report that insights come to them from major Saturn transits that they feel they *could not have had* prior to the event. They have become a subtly different person.

Similarly, while positive thinking and confidence are crucial qualities, always, there is a difference between genuine self-belief and whistling in the dark. Without Saturn's grounding and experience, our attempts to seem assured and worldly wise are like precocious children playing at being grown-ups. Knowledge is of course crucial, but it does not necessarily follow then that fate is averted simply by self-awareness – even the most highly conscious and evolved people are to some extent conditioned by past karma, and while knowledge enables fate to be put into perspective, it does not *automatically* liberate us from further lessons. Integrating Saturnian stuff into our own consciousness involves more than a simple, superficial attitude. It takes time, and definite more or less predetermined events occur before delivery is achieved. Whether these events leave deep scars or rich and valuable experience depends on our own attitude and how we have handled a situation. By facing fear and consciously opening up to dark and initially uncomfortable psychic territory, it is possible to eventually grow more comfortable and in the long term avoid much distress.

The idea of running away from Saturn is often expressed through his hard natal aspects. A square, for instance, from Saturn to any personal planet makes that planet behave in a far more disciplined and constricted fashion. Be it the Sun, Moon, Venus, Mars, whatever, there is an exaggerated sense of duty and decorum that must not be transgressed, and in this area at least, we must keep our self-control. To complain or to look for help outside is weak and contemptible, for we imagine *nobody likes* people who are needy and vulnerable. This stoical attitude may become a source of strength as we grow up, but the intervening time represents a struggle, and a sense of alienation and stress through living life along very tight lines and having to cope on our own. Dignity is never easy. The individual assumes that that he will be rejected by others if he opens up and shows that he can be prone or insecure. But once has built up his ramparts, people really start to turn away because he seems closed and mistrustful and does not give anything away. Then he is properly alone and neatly caught in exactly the kind of syndrome he tried to avoid. Again, fear manifested itself.

True, it is wise sometimes to be discreet, because there are people who will feed on our insecurities. These types are quite rare, however. We are more likely to be harassed or manipulated for as long as our phobias remain hidden, and more likely to actualise enemies or tormenters by fearing them in the first place. Again, if we do not inwardly own our fears, Saturn brings them to life from without. Secrets rattling around underneath our psychic floorboards will probably be heard and eventually exposed, and it goes harder for us the longer they have been confined. The idea that we will be trampled upon if we reveal the slightest self-doubt is in the nature of the anxiety itself. Worries fester and are compounded by refusing to reach out to people and show ourselves. Emotional self-censorship tends to be counter-productive, as we can see from public life. If there is the slightest scandal or controversy, disowning it only creates even bigger curiosity. In any scandal, it is always the secret life or cover-up that arouses greater attention and indignation.

This is not a plea for a kind of narcissistic hypochondria that harps on constantly about its human frailty. There is an admirable side to Saturn's self-reliance, a grown up and responsible attitude that does not like to be a burden to anyone. Owning up to our failings and frailties, we take responsibility for them, and try to move on. Similarly, while we receive much propaganda about the desirability of assertiveness, this too is not for everyone. Shyness and reserve are not fatal flaws. But there are many people with a stressful Saturn in their chart who are quite *painfully* inhibited and simply petrified of feelings, of expressing themselves or speaking out in any way. Saturn sees things in terms of either-or, rather than both-and, yet learns over time that it is possible to be emotionally open at the same time as maintaining a little dignity. A skilful approach to Saturn lies in the balance between maturity, against an excessive reticence that is simply too frightened to reach out.

Of course, some less sensitive types have no discernable tendency whatever to shrink from their Shadow side and embrace their Saturnian darkness quite enthusiastically. 'I'm not here to be popular' is a tough rationale that recognizes a man will not necessarily be everyone's best friend *anyway*, so at least he should ensure a little respect. This is one of Saturn's toughest lessons, one which frequently goes with a leadership position. Deciding what needs to be done for the wider good sometimes means telling people things they do not wish to hear. Refusing this responsibility does not make us any better loved, and does not prevent bad things from happening. Quite often the reverse. The struggle to express Saturn fully is a battle for self-assurance, which is a defining characteristic of many successful people. Problems in life frequently do not come from those who are genuinely confident, but rather the opposite.

The doctrine that we create the world around us by our expectations from day to day has parallels in esoteric thought from all traditions. 'As a man thinketh in his heart, so he becomes'[7]. This idea has become a guiding principle of the whole New Age mission. Saturn is more likely to show fear than love, yet astrology gives us a quite precise and detailed picture of our innate fearful pre-dispositions. It also suggests the means by which we can conquer these fears. In his shadow form, Saturn represents intentions and tendencies that have remained hidden or unacknowledged in our own mind throughout incarnations, and as Jung said, we experience this from the outside as fate. Chronos's myth teaches us love what we have created, and in so doing, shine a light upon our fear.

CHAPTER THREE

MATURE REFLECTION

Saturn's sign and the Inner Adult.

Because of the discomfort usually associated with Saturn, the qualities of his sign placement often take on rather dramatic proportions. A man may brood over them in his quieter moments, building up and magnifying the issues in his mind, until he resembles a person in the presence of someone he is nervous or in awe of. Behaving in the style of our own Saturn feels like walking on a tightrope over a precipice and we feel keenly the absence of a safety net and definitely off our own ground. How to act and what to say? We are shy, self-conscious and compensate by trying to *manage* Saturn's affairs, where it is hard to be spontaneous and go with the flow.

If Saturn is the archetype of maturity, then some of his lessons represent grown up, evolved behaviour in general. Rather than trying to control our environment and relationships, what it comes down to is rather trying to control *ourselves*. Saturn represents the kind of adult attitudes that come after a good deal of experience, and while this is most often associated with chronological age, this is not an exclusive qualification. Commonplace observations about fate have the stamp of Saturn all over them, as with a little maturity we talk about chickens coming home to roost, what goes around comes around, and the importance of being nice to people on the way up, because we meet them again coming down.

The sign position of Saturn is not as significant in practical terms as its house and aspects, but the sign represents the style or 'colour' of Saturn and a personal challenge to surmount. Sign placements represent character and destiny, and of all planets, definite experiences are put in our path, in relation to Saturn's sign. Depending on how easily Saturn sits in the chart, his sign is a fundamental taboo area, or at least a quality treated with respect. These qualities are often disliked, disowned, or projected on to others, but knowing the attributes of our own Saturn should enable us at least to behave more consciously. Saturnian conditioning is among the most deeply rooted attitudes in the horoscope, however, and it is not an easy matter to separate projection from what is real, as if by effort of pure will. We are who we are. The only way to detach entirely from Saturn's influence is either by raising our awareness over a long period of time - or by miraculously becoming somebody else.

Saturn is aspirational however, and there is also a curiosity about his sign; a kind of mystique or fatal attraction that makes it hard to simply sideline his attributes without attempting to express them. As intolerable as they can sometimes seem, we may have a grudging admiration, or envy, for anyone who embodies or articulates our own Saturn qualities in an easy and confident way. We can all 'do' our Saturn sign, but it does not come easily, and certainly, until we embrace Saturn we are less likely to be taken seriously. For this reason, the effort required to own our Saturn qualities means he personifies a kind of confidence and attainment, an image or ideal of maturity. Saturn's sign and to a lesser extent his house placement, show the qualities we consider grown-up.

Aries qualities, ego drive and assertion, which appear so basic and childish to most people, seem impressively adult to the

SATURN IN ARIES character who goes through life apologising for himself. Saturn is traditionally in his 'fall' here, which says something about the discrepancy between Aries's impulsiveness and Saturn's preference for the longer game. While it is a hard-nosed and overbearing character that perhaps springs to mind, the opposite is more often the case. These individuals in fact often lack a basic sense of presence and entitlement and constantly ask themselves: 'What right do I have to speak up, to have desires, to put myself first?' No surprise then that they are marginalized when people think they do not care enough and they may revert to rather boorish behaviour in order to be noticed. Contrarily, Saturn in Aries's potential ruthlessness may be rooted in a fear of confrontation: rather than have an honest exchange, they will try to avoid any hint of a direct face-off by taking an executive decision and acting on their own impulses. Definite shades of Chronos and his children here. Secretly, they wish to show people a powerful side of their character no-one suspects, a hidden Superhero aspect that refuses to take any nonsense. It does not come straight away - they have to lose their temper a few times and be put in a position where push has to come to shove. They eventually learn the difference between aggression and assertion, discovering that life is occasionally a battlefield and the perverse fact that many people actually prefer having their boundaries positively defined.

Somewhat ironically, **Errol Flynn** had this Saturn, closely conjunct his ascendant and perhaps best embodies the Saturn in Aries individual's secret swashbuckling self-image. But fellow Hollywood star, **Jimmy Stewart** is perhaps a better example of the true Saturn in Aries type. Stewart's most famous roles had him as the shy, self-effacing Everyman, who yet possessed a streak of true heroism. This image was apparently not so far from his real-life character.

Aries is also **John Cleese's** Saturn sign and it is easy to see Basil Fawlty as the Aries shadow personified. Basil's frustrations in fact stem from his desire for a quiet life, and his manic outbursts come about through the Saturn in Aries nightmare - trying unsuccessfully to assert himself. Sybil is actually the assured, authoritative one at Fawlty Towers, of whom everyone ultimately takes notice.

Fyodor Dostoyevsky, Albert Einstein, Oskar Schindler, Lee Harvey Oswald, Rudolph Nureyev, Germaine Greer, Jack Nicklaus, Marvin Gaye, Michael Schumacher, Nicole Kidman. *The Wizard of Oz* (movie).

SATURN IN TAURUS seems about as materialistic a placement as can be imagined, though imagination does not always come into it. Nothing that cannot be tasted, touched, smelled, heard or seen can be quite trusted, and ephemeral notions of intuition and imagination are treated with suspicion. Wrestling with this idea, the Saturn in Taurus individual has potential to build and create in an artistic sense: working with basic earthy materials in a typically Saturnian way. These folk make a virtue of commonsense and down to earth values, while their ideal of maturity is to be materially self sufficient, if not a major financial player. There may also be a sense of guilt attached to this goal, with their innate awareness of the ephemeral nature of money bringing an accompanying fear that their resources will one day simply evaporate. Conversely, some have an aversion to excessively bourgeois trappings of wealth or status, preferring to live a simpler, more Spartan lifestyle, idealising the ascetic who does not need material badges of success. Typically, these two conditions see-saw side by side, until the Saturn Taurus person eventually reaches a Middle Way. Realising that while money does not buy happiness, neither does *no* money and the longed-for security that they seek exists inside themselves.

This is the Saturn placement of the wise **Professor Richard Dawkins**, best-selling pop-science author and the self-styled scourge of astrology. One of his recurring themes is we do not need mysticism if (like him, no doubt) we fully understand the world around us in all its infinite complexity. However, given the bizarre fact that no public pronouncement from this high secular priest of materialism seems to be complete without a sideswipe at astrology, we might speculate that he protests too much and in fact harbours a secret fascination for mysticism and the study of the stars.

Nicolo Machiavelli was in many ways a defining Saturnian figure. Saturn in Taurus ruling his Capricorn ascendant represented his ambition, but more a kind of ruthless, earthy pragmatism. Machiavelli has become notorious for 'the dictator's defence', his doctrine that the ends justify the means, but this was only the first overt Saturnian statement of the guiding principle of politics ever since his time.

Emily Bronte, Vincent Van Gogh, Louis Pasteur, Pablo Picasso, Richard Nixon, Muhammad Ali, John Lennon, Al Pacino, *Monty*

Python's Flying Circus.

SATURN IN GEMINI individuals demand to do their own thinking. Early on in their lives, they might struggle in classroom situations, when their refusal to conform with received wisdom is seen as perversity or outright stupidity. As they grow up, however and their innovative investigations achieve more respect, they are more accurately seen as intellectual connoisseurs whose original in-depth analysis explodes many misguided myths. Conscious of their own weighty mentality, they have an aversion to glib Geminian clever-cleverness, insisting instead on thoroughly thought-out, internally consistent theories that stand the test of time. There is a danger here of over-intellectualising everything: the 'that's all very well in practice, how does it work in theory?' syndrome. Their ideal is of the mature scientist or thinker, who has *looked into* matters and whose intellectual exposition opens up previously obscure or inelegantly expressed information.

No birth time is recorded for **Roger Waters**, Pink Floyd's principle songwriter, but it appears that he has an unaspected Saturn in Gemini. Unmodified or influenced by any other horoscope factors, unaspected planets are not integrated into the rest of the chart, and function in a 'pure', either-or fashion. Certainly, Waters' preoccupations seem very Saturnian, from *The Dark Side of The Moon* to *The Wall*, a concept album dealing with strangeness and alienation. Emerging in Waters' twenty-ninth year, 1972's *Dark Side* is a characteristically Saturn return album, dealing with themes of time, death and madness – a nod perhaps towards Saturn in Gemini. All this was done while achieving a remarkable austere and time*less* Saturnian musical style.

Jerry Springer began his career as a lawyer and political aide to Robert Kennedy, before running unsuccessfully for Congress in his own right. He eventually found his Saturn in Gemini niche as a tabloid TV presenter, treating serious subjects in a comic and highly sensationalised style.

King George III of England, Sigmund Freud, John Maynard Keynes, Rupert Sheldrake, Vivienne Leigh, Brian Wilson, Bobby Fischer, Jimi Hendrix.

With its natural rulership of the Mother and family, Cancer's issues evoke mixed emotions in most people, but the **SATURN IN CANCER** individual always imagines his background is more embarrassing than anyone else's. His family is seen as something to live down, holding him back from his own plans and self-expression. While sometimes there may be a strong, dutiful connection here, a desire to be his own person also results in a kind of arms-length familial relationship, making an exaggerated point of the nobility of independence. Escaping from the skeletons of their own ancestry, these individuals are determined to establish their personal family with entirely different values. However, there is also a kind of aspiration and idealisation of the family unit, perhaps very deeply buried, and those who share a strong clannish connection may be perceived in a very mature light. The parental image may be quite forbidding: an overpowering maternal figure or stern patriarch, but it is an image of maturity for the person with this Saturn.

Britain, in many ways very Saturnian country, has several great patriots with Saturn in Cancer. Though he never actually spoke the famous lines attributed to him on the eve of Agincourt, **King Henry V** inspired **Shakespeare** to these heights of patriotic bombast. Shakespeare himself had this Saturn, if we believe his traditional birth time, and **Elizabeth I,** too. **Dr Samuel Johnson** was also a member of the Saturn in Cancer clan, and for some reason: 'Patriotism is the last refuge of a scoundrel' has become his best-known quotation. Perhaps there is a timeless truth in the remark, and anyone with Saturn in this sign is bound to see nationalism of any sort in a rather dubious light, but it is ironic coming from an Englishman famed for his own rather parochial (not to say xenophobic) attitudes. Composer **Sir Edward Elgar** also had this Saturn, and his *Pomp and Circumstance March* has become the embodiment of flag-waving jingoism, and *Nimrod,* the soundtrack of essential Englishness.

Michelangelo, George Bernard Shaw, DH Lawrence, Yehudi Menhuin, John F. Kennedy, Frank Sinatra, Bob Marley, Leonardo DiCaprio.

A person with **SATURN IN LEO** looks up to anyone who can express themselves easily and hold the attention of a room. Their mature ideal is the confident, accomplished person who pulls everything off effortlessly and with a certain flair. Fearing being overlooked, the Saturn Leo person is diffident about showing their need to be appreciated and may have, at best, a sneaking regard for others who are able to be flamboyant and effusive. There is a feeling of being never quite great enough, always reaching for more praise and achievement, and while they fear mediocrity, they also feel it rather invidious to show their natural, easy self-expression. Or out of frustration with, or a reaction against the desire for status and acclaim, this may also be described as the anti-hero or 'punk placement'[8] of Saturn, where the individual wishes for notoriety and seeks attention for ugly and perverse reasons. There can be of course a charming modesty about Saturn in Leos – they can do pizzazz, but it is not enough to make a hollow show of their creativity, they have a strong need for something substantive to back it up with. This, they first of all have to prove to themselves, which in a shallow, celebrity-obsessed culture is pretty refreshing.

This is **Freddie Mercury's** Saturn. There are several notable performers of his generation born with Saturn and Pluto conjunct, who are lucky enough to have a kind of alter ego to live out their outrageous side. Freddie was the epitome of camp, flamboyant showmanship, though offstage he was apparently shy and reserved.

But it is Nelson Mandela, with Saturn conjunct Mercury in Leo who supplies the definitive credo for this placement, so much so that it begs to be given in full:

"Our deepest fear is not that we are inadequate. Our deepest fear is that we are powerful beyond measure. It is our light, not our darkness, that frightens us most. We ask ourselves, "Who am I to be brilliant, gorgeous, talented, and famous?" Actually, who are you not to be? You are a child of God. Your playing small does not serve the world. There is nothing enlightened about shrinking so that people won't feel insecure around you. We were born to make manifest the glory of God that is within us. It's not just in some of us; it's in all of us. And when we let our own light shine, we unconsciously give other people permission to do the same. As we are liberated from our own fear, our presence automatically liberates others."

This quote comes from a mature man approaching his *third* Saturn return, who has meditated on these matters for a long time. It is so utterly revealing about Saturn in Leo, and one senses that he has wrestled throughout his life with precisely the doubts and insecurities that he speaks of. There are lessons in his words for any placement of Saturn.

Eleanor of Aquitaine, Thomas Jefferson, Beethoven, Leo Tolstoy, Chiang Kai-Shek, Bill Clinton, Elton John, Stephen Spielberg

SATURN IN VIRGO demands perfection and order, though there may equally be a reaction against it. They would dearly like to live up to the advertising agency's idealised image of the perfectly healthy, spic-and-span executive who works out at the health club before hitting the office at 7:30 prompt, with their sparkling teeth, immaculate suit and costly watch. Virgo embodies this search for perfection – a healthy mind in a healthy body, with a spotlessly ordered and idealised routine, all ready to provide perfect, selfless service. Saturn desperately wishes to share in this notion, but is brought up against the fact that such perfect ideas do not allow for the apparent randomness and chaos of everyday life, where the traffic is bad, the trains are late and, sorry, there is a temporary fault on the line. Finding sensible, intelligent, fine-tuned solutions may in fact be Saturn's forte here, but life is not a chessboard and logic is not commonsense. The wisdom of this position is in working around the need for perfect order and finding achievable, real-world answers.

Lewis Carrol had this Saturn position, retrograde, and no-one has better illustrated the absurdities of language and life and the folly of trying making the world fit a logical pre-ordained plan than the creator of Alice, Humpty-Dumpty and the Mad Hatter.

Poet and philosopher **Samuel Taylor Coleridge** had Saturn in Virgo, conjunct Venus in the Ninth house. The famous Romantic ran away to the army at the age of twenty to escape his debts, where he provided essential Virgoan service by writing love letters for the other soldiers to send home to their wives.

Bruce Springsteen's signature songs celebrate the blue-collar worker in true Saturn in Virgo style. Saturn's fourth house placement also represents Springsteen's lyrical preoccupation with everyday heroes and heroines' search to escape their small-town backgrounds.

JS Bach, Rene Descartes, Agatha Christie, Groucho Marx, Prince Charles, Timothy Leary, Richard Branson.

SATURN IN LIBRA people are the politicians and diplomats of the zodiac. They see the wisdom of maturity in the peacemaker and this is the ideal to which they aspire. While there may be dissatisfaction with their own partnership, they admire those who can build bridges and come to creative compromises. There is much value in this, as suggested by Saturn's exaltation here, though the excessive reliance on the general other party is often in no-one's interests. Sharing may be seen as compromise, and they feel compro*mised* as a result. The usual attraction-repulsion with Saturn's placement may be found, and these people have a hard time deciding whether to go it alone or put everything to the committee. They learn that leadership may involve a measure of manipulation and individual credit has to be foregone sometimes for the interests of the wider good - or that is what they tell themselves. Very often it is the opposite way around, with Saturn in Libra's ringing declaration of altruistic intent forming a convenient smokescreen for their own agenda. As has been mentioned, the sign of the Scales has a natural resonance with The Lord of Karma, and handling Saturn successfully revolves invariably around finding a golden medium.

Oliver Cromwell is seen either as the champion of British Parliamentary tradition, or a vicious and ruthless autocrat. Natal Saturn opposite Mars in Aries signified his soldier-statesman status, manifesting in his undoubted military skill, but also in his bloody subjugation, even by the brutal standards of his day. With archetypal Saturnian irony, after the execution of Charles I, this most radical Republican ended up as Lord Protector of England; King in all but name. This transformation from revolutionary leader to eventual despot is the perfect embodiment of the myth of Chronos.

Bob Geldof is a Sun Libran with an exalted Saturn, and he has become known as a kind of maverick pop-politician for his unconventional methods of money and consciousness-raising. Despite his undoubted gift for bringing people together, his passion and commitment manifest as a kind of shadowy Libran rudeness and belligerence.

Richard the Lionheart, Richard III of England, Leonardo Da Vinci, Jane Austen, Mao Tse Tsung, Henry Ford, Henry Kissinger, Judy Garland, Norman Mailer, Christopher Reeve.

SATURN IN SCORPIO has an innate nervousness about visceral, deep down issues of sex and sharing. Such matters are considered 'not nice' and better left alone, and while this may be a sensible attitude in many cases, there is no ultimate hiding place from Scorpio stuff and circumstances gently compel these individuals to open their eyes. Scorpio governs release from the physical world and transcendence through sex, though Saturn makes all of this seem rather scary – which, no doubt, intense, passionate encounters may be. One defence against this is switching to the opposite extreme: affecting a kind of indifference around intimacy, a cool and blasé attitude that masks their true feelings. So this may be someone with no inhibitions in bed, for example, but who does not like holding hands. An early precocity around sex may leave ambivalent attitudes later in life, or experiences that take some time to process and fully understand. There is a sense of decorum here, of things which are better left alone, and squeamishness about any issue that lies beneath surface appearances. Still, they may see those who are genuinely comfortable about sex and intimacy as being very mature and together.

This is **Oprah Winfrey's** Saturn sign, the woman who took taboo, psychological issues into prime-time television. Sexually abused for many years as a child, she overcame her profoundly difficult background in spectacular style to become almost a byword for a form of popular, confessional self-analysis, and also one of the richest and most influential women in America.

Hugh Hefner, *Playboy's* founder, has Saturn in Scorpio in the Third house. His publishing empire has been built on sexual fantasy, establishing an aspirational, pseudo-sophisticated male lifestyle to measure up to. No surprise perhaps that 'Hef' came from a puritanical, Church-oriented background, with apparently very cold, undemonstrative parents.

Mary Queen of Scots, Goethe, Mark Twain, Rudyard Kipling, Fidel Castro, Marlon Brando, Marilyn Monroe, Miles Davis, Annie Lennox.

SATURN IN SAGITTARIUS struggles with basic faith and optimism, unsure of whether life will provide or whether to prepare for the worst. There is nothing inherently atheistic about this placement, but there is still a deep ambivalence toward formal religious belief, which carries the oppressive and life-denying Saturn projection. Some may be found in various places of worship, partaking in the outward trappings and rituals of faith, *wishing* that they believed, because it is the grown up thing. Others may have the 'devout sceptic' syndrome: quoting scriptural chapter and verse and utilising the powerful language, attitudes and imagery of religion, without actually having made their own leap of faith. At first resenting or patronising those with belief in spiritual things, over time, the Saturn Sagittarius person may accept there is something to the whole matter and wishes to share in it. At this point, atheistic arguments no longer have much sway, for they are precisely the kind of opinions they themselves used to hold. There is no sceptic like the priest. Their faith is lasting and based on true reflection and experience, not tradition, superstition or book learning, which is the difference between true knowledge, and unthinking piety or blind faith.

A surprising number of modern religious cum political martyrs have had Saturn in Sagittarius: **Abraham Lincoln, Rasputin, Gandhi, Martin Luther King, Chè Guevara.** All of these romantic, charismatic personalities were acutely controversial in their time, and all were assassinated. Politics and religion seemed to be bound up in their fate, and their message and presence stirred up a reaction so powerful that it became necessary for their enemies to kill them. **Osama Bin Laden** is a modern day zealot who bids fair to continue the martyrdom signature.

Many musicians seem innately spiritual and **Madonna** is a classic case of a seeker who has discovered a fitting religious vehicle in the Kabala. Brought up a practicing Catholic, she has spoken at length of her need to find something more fulfilling than the merely material.

(Bonny) Prince Charles Stuart, Humphrey Bogart, Enzo Ferrari, Alfred Hitchcock, Al Capone, Gabriel Garcia Marquez, Prince (musician).

SATURN IN CAPRICORN is in his own sign and has an

easier time fitting in with the Saturnian archetype of the influential achiever, but these are the qualities to which people with this placement aspire. Success for its own sake is the quality sought out here, however the Saturn Capricorn person defines it. The image is of a grown up, a dignified man of affairs who does not overreach himself but keeps a sensible knowledge of his own boundaries. Limitations apply here in terms of time too: the Saturn in Capricorn type is not fazed by the prospect of a lengthy campaign of hard work stretching out over the years, as long as the eventual goal is kept in sight. Worldly ambition is usually assured, but even those who are not in the material success game demand to live life on their own terms, without compromise. Taken to extremes of course this leads to a pushy, sharp-elbowed ambition, and an unsentimental willingness to use any expedient measure to get ahead. Just as gravely, there may be an exaggeratedly goal-oriented existence where all gratification has been deferred and life has not been fully lived and cherished in the moment. More commonly, however, those with Saturn in Capricorn do not wish to control anyone else, as long as they feel they are their *own* boss.

This is **Clint Eastwood's** Saturn, who has built a whole career on playing the sardonic, self-reliant anti-hero. In the movie *Magnum Force*, his running line is: 'A good man's *got* to know his limitations'. Clint bought the rights to his 1992 movie *Unforgiven* many years before he made the film, then waited until he was old enough to credibly play the lead role - and in the same year rode off with the Best Director Oscar. This is an example of a positive Saturn.

Kevin Spacey is another Oscar-spangled Hollywood hero with an eye for the longer game. In 2003, he became Artistic Director of London's Old Vic theatre, aiming to restore the 200-year old venue to its former glories. Poor critical reviews of his early productions have not deterred Saturn-in Capricorn Spacey, who has said he intends to remain in the high-pressure and high profile post for at least ten years.

Charles Dickens, Immanuel Kant, Voltaire, Henry James, Walt Disney, Mikhael Gorbachev, Rupert Murdoch, Sylvia Plath.

Those with **SATURN IN AQUARIUS** are usually uncomfortable about revealing their different or unorthodox side. Yet they are as quirky and idiosyncratic as anybody, and possibly more than most. There is a great shyness about standing out from the crowd, even when it is obvious to everyone that they are not Mr or Mrs Normal. A common ploy is for them to portray an almost exaggeratedly conventional lifestyle; steady job, cosy relationship, semi in the suburbs, while keeping their left-field activities (veganism, radical politics, Kabbalah,) well behind the scenes. Saturn is of course at home in Aquarius and there is merit in their subtly conservative side, and in not deviating too far from established norms. There is also great potential to put a new twist on an old idea and keep some classic concept ahead of the times. This is a potentially statesmanlike position of Saturn, slow to change, though like the politician, they insist on their own innovations and their ideals may turn into edicts over the passage of time. Their mature ideal is of the public figure or prophet who dreams of making the world a better place, ironically through daring to speak out and be different. Fear of seeming eccentric or out of step holds them back, though if anything, it is this excessively conformist outlook that may make them look slightly silly.

The political aspect and enforced conformity of Saturn in Aquarius, is *1984* made real, so no surprise that this is **George Orwell's** Saturn. Here is not so much the nightmare of intrusion and surveillance, but of the State gone mad, with all individual expression outlawed. Orwell's exact Sun-Moon-Neptune conjunction may have something to say about his own vision of Room 101, but it is with a jolt sometimes that we see a chart that expresses the archetype of a given astrological point so precisely

.

Marsilio Ficino, William Blake, Charlotte Bronte, Winston Churchill, Carl Jung, Greta Garbo, Georgio Armani, Elvis Presley, Johnny Depp.

Saturn rules boundaries and doorways and Pisces rules the infinite, so **SATURN IN PISCES** makes a quite intriguing match. This person starts off with an innate mistrust of the irrational, intuitive and sacrificial, though the wise mystic or expert healer may be set up as a mature ideal. The basic paradox here of attempting to put the boundless within limits explains their fear and discomfort of confinement, and perhaps a basic unwillingness to be emotionally hemmed in. Saturn is the material world and Pisces is about spirit, so this person *believes* up to a certain point, but while a mystical world-view may be entertained, they also want solid ground under their feet. The image is rather like the cartoon character running off the edge of a cliff, and only falling when he looks down. Churches or other spiritual institutions are usually treated with distrust until the individual has subjected it to their own rigorous scrutiny. Good. There is so much rubbish written and said about spiritual and psychic phenomena that a little healthy scepticism is a rare commodity, and the Saturn Pisces person is unlikely to buy into any of this stuff blind, without first giving its tyres a fairly firm kick.

Kurt Cobain was a Sun Pisces, with Saturn also in the sign of the Fishes, opposite Pluto. Pitiful as it is to include anyone famous principally for destroying himself, Cobain stands as the embodiment of a kind of hopeless romantic nihilism. This is an extreme and chilling example of Saturn in Pisces, but someone who it seemed could not be happy, no matter how objectively fortunate.

    Sir Isaac Newton had this position of Saturn. Aptly enough for the architect of the mechanistic universe, he transformed the mysterious forces of nature into clear and understandable terms with his mathematical laws of gravity and motion. Even more appropriately, this truly Saturnian genius formulated the law of karma as an equation: 'to every action there is an equal and opposite reaction'. His famous retort to Edmund Halley may have been apocryphal, but: 'I have studied it' is still the correct response to anyone asking if we believe in astrology.

Sir Walter Raleigh, Queen Victoria, Alexander Graham Bell, Jean-Paul Sartre, Edgar Cayce, Woody Allen, Jack Nicholson, Russell Crowe.

CHAPTER FOUR

CROSSROADS BLUES
Saturn transiting the planets

Like no other heavenly body, transiting Saturn determines the difference between good times and bad in life; times when everything is sweet and clear and passages that are oppressed and weighed down, for no outwardly apparent reason. Once again it is Saturn that seems to make the difference between happiness and misery. Without knowledge of astrology, there are just good days and bad, up times and down, with no further insight into why events, moods, passions, accidents and windfalls happen at given times, or why life is in either the doldrums or a mini golden age. Whether we co-operate with our limitations or attempt to burst through, raging against fate probably depends on our natal chart. It also depends on time and the wisdom we eventually learn in relation to our own Saturn.

Hard transiting aspects from Saturn tend to produce events and manifestation, because we feel compelled to act and adjust. This may not be either a very welcome or a comfortable experience, but these transits leave behind them solid achievements and hopefully a lasting legacy. New jobs or relationships, a new direction or ambitions begin under Saturn's auspices, most frequently the conjunction, square or opposition. This is when the new initiative takes place, though the harvest or crowning achievement more often arrives under a transiting trine. Most noticeable are Saturn's transits to the Sun and Moon, in relation to self- expression and emotional life respectively. These, especially the conjunction and opposition, are among the most important of all transits, and certainly the most powerful and perceptible, both in their immediate impact and their lasting effect.

Rule one on page one of the astrologer's handbook is that nothing shall come to pass that is not promised in the natal chart. Planetary transits are simply the unfolding of the birth map over a life, and the resonance of natal aspects carry into the transiting experience. The condition of a given planet, good or ill, determines how easily the transiting challenge is met. A natal chart full of soft aspects receives much apparent good fortune without a great deal of effort and the life path seems smooth and unruffled. Equally, individuals with 'easy charts' have a broad comfort zone and may give up or go to pieces at the first sign of a struggle. These types are more likely to keep within their proscribed limits, and content with a certain level of achievement, see no reason to challenge fate and stretch themselves further. Someone with a domineering natal Saturn in a chart full of awkward angles on the other hand, is more likely to regard fate's glass ceiling as no obstacle.

So it is not *the* planets that are transited, it is *our* planets: not Venus or *the* Moon, but *our* Venus and *our* Moon. Still, hard transiting aspects from *our* Saturn are likely to roughen up the edges even of a planet that is in super shape. Again, it can go harder for us in times of trouble if we do not have the essential conditioning of a few difficult natal aspects to ensure we only bend and do not break. Whenever Saturn hits a planet, it is also like partaking of that natal aspect for a while. When transiting Saturn opposes the Sun, for instance, we discover what it is like to have this aspect at birth, to feel challenged with the sense that we have a great deal to live up to. Saturn hitting the Moon on the other hand, puts us in the shoes of the individual who learned early on that it is no good crying to mother. All these transits are priceless entries in the notebook of a consulting astrologer who needs to empathise with his or her clients' experience.

Under any Saturn transit, depending on the orientation of a given chart, the lessons can either take the form of material events: job loss or promotion, new relationship, bankruptcy, parenthood, moving house, emigrating, or mental/ spiritual insights. Clearly, one begets the other, though it is not so clear which side, material or psychological, is the tougher. Losing a job, for instance can be catastrophic, but it is perhaps not so bad if we hated what we were doing. On the other hand, somebody realising that they are in the wrong line of work, or that they have held themselves back for many years through a fear of success, for example, may find this harder to deal with. The same applies to a relationship. A partner walking out can be one of the hardest things anyone has to bear, but realising that we have lived with certain expectations or wrong, severely limiting assumptions is not necessarily easier. Such sea-change insights are tied in to events, though not exclusively. It may take a material change to trigger the realisation; an apparent setback that forces us to think differently. But the Saturn transit often *is* the event, a profound psychic change that has a corresponding effect on our body and environment.

We can also understand transits as either causes or signs. Rather than seeing transiting Saturn as *creating* events from without, it is better in practical terms to see him as a *signpost* suggesting the appropriate kind of action or inner attitude to embrace at a given time. This is an important distinction. Instead of being passive, sleeping partners in a transit, it is better to enlist our imagination and try participating in the symbolism. Of all planets, Saturn is the one most likely to bring the intervention of fate without any apparent antecedence in our own actions, and we may also regret the lack of spontaneity represented by second-guessing our every move according to the ephemeris. But this is all the more reason to keep on our toes. The individual who consciously looks for a post teaching abroad before Saturn hits his Ninth house Jupiter, for example, is surely a step ahead of the game, and is more likely to get an easier ride from the conditions of the time. We can either *happen to* the transit, or have the transit *happen* to us.

We may be especially imaginative and devise more *lateral* ways of expressing the *literal* tendency of Saturn. Bear in mind that he inevitably involves work of some sort, and also a twist of fate, and a transit that lets us off lightly is more likely happy chance than any cunning plan on our part. At the same time, working honestly at Saturn is a way of cultivating such serendipity. There is a kind of alchemy that takes place once a particular challenge is accepted, which also makes the task intrinsically lighter and less daunting, not to mention the material rewards and the eventual sense of freedom. The harder we work, the luckier we get.

TRANSITING SATURN IN ASPECT

Conjunctions of Saturn to any planet put the spotlight squarely upon it and the house that it occupies. It is the start of a new cycle of growth; a rebirth of sorts, but equally a difficult delivery. There may need to be a reorganisation and cutting away in order to promote new expansion. Saturn is like lead, a dense, crushing experience, yet anything that survives the impact is likely to be solid and worth sticking with. This applies to career paths, friendships, homes, marriages; everything. Along with the need for hard work, there is often a feeling of time passing, particularly with Saturn's transits to itself, and also the Sun. There is a tangible, fundamental change. We may appear older and in the immediate term somewhat pessimistic, though people are tough and can usually adjust to any change and soon it becomes the norm. Tougher characters may find Saturn conjunctions simply put them on their mettle and inspire them to set up solid, lasting structures that endure for years.

Transiting **squares** by Saturn to any planet are like a health check for our ambitions, a short-term stop, where the individual analyses where he is going in the longer term. Squares are always challenging and can bring sharp reminders of what we should be doing in relation to a given planet's affairs, but assuming there was a major re-orientation at the conjunction or opposition point, nothing drastic should need doing. The effects are troubling, but not generally life-changing. If anything is wrong in our overall direction, it is like being pulled over by the karma police for having a flat tire or an unfastened safety belt, not for anything serious. After being flagged down, the cosmic authorities wave us on without a word. Some astrologers insist that squares are tougher than oppositions, because the two planets are not facing each other in plain sight. The planetary protagonists are in each other's peripheral vision and the whole business is more obscure and unconscious. Square aspects show planets at odds with each other – we can have either A or B, but not A and B together, and this is especially marked by squares from Saturn. To 'square' things means to reconcile.

Saturn's transiting **trines** are usually very rewarding. The rewards or openings we receive do not necessarily appear particularly glamorous, but there is a breakthrough nevertheless if we have put effort in and not backed down. Rather than the latest toy or fashion accessory, Saturn's gift is something solid and practical that will last a long time. Small acorns grow at this point and our faith, hard work and persistence pay off to create solid, lasting situations. We have chiselled away patiently and the wall or obstacle in our path comes crashing down. This truly represents the best of Saturn, and in many ways the best of any transiting planet, precisely because the rewards are paid in fine, durable quality. There is no trade-off between duty and leisure, work and play. There is greater potential for self-determination and we have a cool, measured approach to the affairs of any planet.

The **sextile** is very similar to the trine, only subtler. Doors do not fling themselves wide open under transiting sextiles, but a crack appears just wide enough for us to get a toe in. We prepare the ground for the future and a window of opportunity appears. Appreciating the nature of the goal, we start warming to our task. Everything is growing and there is a sense of anticipation, brought to a head by the eventual harvest, represented by the trine.

The **opposition** of Saturn to any planet is a watershed phase, a make or break experience. We feel tested and stretched and there is a feeling of being out on a limb. Unlike the transiting square, the questions raised are more fundamental and may represent a major turning point in a life. Saturn pulls hard in a different direction to the planet he opposes, and this frequently brings the *coup de grace* for any enterprise that has limped along with increasing frustration and steadily diminishing returns. The fact that Saturn is at his furthest point from a planet also lends us a sense of perspective. Oppositions are aspects of relationship and these are the times when we can see ourselves most clearly, and understand exactly what needs doing in relation to a given planet's affairs. We may not *like* what we see, but it becomes obvious if anything needs to be done. The analogy with an opposition is the full Moon, a time of fulfilment and harvest, and some very strong personalities may find this extreme tension brings out their best qualities.

Light and Shade: Saturn-Sun transits.

The Sun represents the individual's outward sense of identity and means of self-expression. In tropical astrology it is the central planet, the life-giving force and soul of the horoscope, and this status is perversely reinforced by Saturn's transits. There is nothing quite like a transiting Saturn conjunction or opposition to remind us of how essential a healthy Sun is when all is otherwise well. The difference in the individual's manner, outward behaviour and attitude and lifestyle are often quite marked and such transits signify staging posts in life, arguably as much as Saturn's transits to itself. The effect of Saturn's conjunction and opposition to the Sun, is often apparent to other people, as well as to ourselves while experiencing the transit. Both the Saturn-Sun conjunction and opposition are among the most important times in a life.

The conjunction feels like a new beginning. Embarking upon aims and ambitions signified by the house position of natal Sun, it feels like life has to be reconstructed from the ground up. It is as though an enormous weight has dropped from the sky, and we have to catch it and run with it, truly bearing it on our shoulders for a while. A sense of added onus makes the individual appear varyingly mature, responsible, old for his years and perhaps rather careworn. The usual bright self-expression of the Sun goes behind a cloud for a while and a man may enter into a period of deferred gratification. There is so much to do, with little time for enjoyment or light-hearted distractions. Even when not actually at work, we seem preoccupied with the future and weighty matters, without being able to switch off. People often dress down at this time and may appear rather frumpy or functional in their clothes, with plain utilitarian outfits that do them no particular favours. This is either a sign of a lacklustre state of mind, or that our energies are concentrated elsewhere and we do not feel like making much of an effort.

Though physical energy is often low, a dutiful, hardworking attitude can bring spectacular results. With the right aims and ambition, this is one of the times in life where we actually do something about our dreams, rather than airily talking about them in abstract terms. While this may not be altogether pleasurable at the time, we can look back afterwards with satisfaction. This is a prime example of Saturn laying down a challenge and rather than simply letting us drift along, he grabs us by the collar and demands action. The goals and ambitions worked towards should be for the long term – the transit is tough enough without settling for short-term options. Once again, hard work is a magic mantra at this time and it is somewhat in the nature of Saturn that as soon as his issues are worked on and there is a positive *willingness* to act, then doors miraculously start to open: only an inch at a time, perhaps, but wide enough to get a foot in. Once again, facing the fear is the key.

The Saturn-Sun opposition is similar in its effects, except rather than dropping directly upon our head, the lead weight of Saturn seems to fall somewhere in front, blocking our present lane on the highway. There is an enormous obstacle in our path, casting a great shadow and we have to decide how we are going to get over or around it, or whether to turn around and try a different road altogether. Oppositions are aspects of relationship and the symbolic boulder blocking the individual's progress is often embodied by Saturnian characters; bosses, higher-ups and authority figures who are unsympathetic to his cause. This highlights both the issues of the house of the natal Sun and the opposing house that transiting Saturn occupies. This is definitely a time for cutting losses. Any ambition that has not worked out or is proving uneconomical in terms of effort should not be pursued indefinitely. No matter how low our morale, or how many apparent setbacks we have suffered, we should have enough imagination to realise that our present circumstances are *not* the very best they can be. It feels hard to make new endeavours, but still more reason to keep faith with what we are doing and appreciate that things can and will get better.

This is another defining transit, inasmuch as the point where Saturn is furthest away from the Sun and symbolically demarks the outer boundaries of our world. The Saturnian corridor we are following becomes narrower, though this is not always a bad thing. After this transit, rather than seeing ambitions as endless vistas stretching out into infinity, our focus becomes more refined and specialised. Mundanely, this is often a time when people become aware of certain limitations in their lives: instead of trying to take on all comers and become a world-conquering superhero, they may decide on more personal, gratifying and achievable goals. This may mean setting up a business instead of working in a large corporation to make someone else rich. Or rather than trying to seduce everybody we meet, or holding out for the Perfect Relationship, we have a Saturnian reality check and decide to settle down and get married.

Though it is only half the cycle, Saturn's opposition to the Sun *feels* like a full-circle experience. The sense of time having passed is very strong and people often feel older than their years, no matter what chronological age at the time. During the transit itself, physical energy is at an all-time low and we feel weary and perhaps resistant to change. This is only the immediate effect, however: the lasting impact is far more significant – to an almost equal effect as the Saturn return itself, what we want after the Saturn-Sun opposition is not the same as what we wanted before. It is an organic point and afterwards we feel like different people.

The Tough and the Tender: Saturn-Moon transits

Saturn and the Moon do not sit comfortably together – each does badly in the other's sign and in many ways they represent opposing sides of life. Saturn relates to the outer world, while the Moon of course is the inner, emotional life. Saturn finds that feelings simply get in the way, while the soft-centred Moon suffers under the grinding Saturnian desire for work and achievement. Wherever these two connect, there are issues to do with security and self-sufficiency. Saturn-Moon transits are about emotional growing-up experiences. Hard transiting aspects mean that some external emotional support we have used can no longer be relied upon, and we are thrown back on our own inner resources. Transiting trines and sextiles on the other hand mean that we can accomplish this more easily – we grow into ourselves gracefully and find alternative means of security and support. While these two planets are essentially inimical to one another, like a marriage or a parent-child relationship they have to find some means of accommodation.

In truth, this is where emotional growing pains can really kick in. Inasmuch as Saturn-Sun transits make us appreciate how much we rely on the Sun for self-expression, Saturn hitting the Moon is a reminder that inner wellbeing is absolutely integral to happiness. The Moon is the underlying filter through which emotions are assimilated, and works in deep-rooted, all pervading way. During turbulent lunar moments, it is hard to imagine ever having inner peace or feeling content ever again. The problem is not the outside world, but the way we perceive it, and there appears to be no prospect of relief. The Moon says: 'I can't help how I feel', to which Saturn coolly responds: 'we are more than our feelings'. The struggle to reconcile these two views can be among the most uncomfortable of all.

An analogy for Saturn-Moon transits of all kinds is the formal family occasion. The relatives are gathered together in all their finery, and there is a sense of honouring the roots of the tribe and being around our familiars. But there is a trade off between the formality and dutiful nature of the day and the sense of togetherness it is supposed to celebrate. Almost inevitably, there are awkward moments and recollections at such times, as the past comes around to haunt us, and we have to reconcile how far we identify with the background we have come from. Easy, supportive Saturn-Moon transits are where the party is going well: happy rites of passage where there is no conflict between the past and present and we can demonstrate what strong, independent people we have become. Challenging aspects between Saturn and the Moon on the other hand represent a scenario where the formal occasion outweighs the emotional bond it is there to honour. There is a slightly hollow, alienated feeling and skeletons from the family closet come out and make an awkward atmosphere.

Every lunar relationship carries with it a suggestion of the Mother or the archetypal feminine. This is a point where the individual's relationship with feminine figures comes under scrutiny. Someone we have relied on for comfort and support is no longer so available and we must find some other way of getting our emotional needs met. Or we are the ones taking responsibility and providing sympathy, as someone around us needs assurance and assistance. Elderly relatives are an archetypal case in point, tugging on our heartstrings as well as possibly requiring physical care. This may be done willingly or unwillingly, but there is an inevitable sense of duty somewhere in the scenario. Saturn conjoining the Moon especially makes us feel emotionally dry and parched, like a plant that needs watering. It could, or even should, however, be a time to start establishing greater security in the sense of domestic roots and ties.

The opposition tends to be a time when Saturn's issues have pulled us too far out of a sense of emotional centeredness and a reorientation is in order. Working too hard, staying out too much, not eating well, this is one of the most stressful and potentially upsetting transits of all. There may be a sense of alienation, from home, roots and family, or simply from our own selves: working so hard that there is no chance to rest, reflect or repair. There may be a physical alienation, in the sense of being actually separated from roots and loved ones, or a more psychic schism where the individual cannot connect with people, due to arguments, misunderstandings or adverse circumstances. Even in familiar surroundings, we feel a long way from home. It is essential for anyone to be nice to themselves at this time, not work too hard or pile unnecessary pressure on. The potential reward is of greater inner strength, and of finding a sense of home and belonging wherever we happen to be.

Easy aspects between Saturn and the Moon suggest a more refined and comfortable means of combining structure with emotion. These are the times when we realise we have grown up and have the opportunity to show our new maturity. We can have the family ties and duty calls, but not at the expense of genuine feeling and a sense of emotional warmth. We do not allow ourselves to be emotionally pressured or manipulated. Regardless of our own sex, we may get support from a mature person, perhaps an older woman in the classic Saturn-Moon sense. The individual can make his or her own choices about emotional responsibilities rather than blindly having them enforced from the outside.

Mind over Matter: Saturn-Mercury transits

Saturn transiting natal Mercury is where the individual's thoughts and ideas start to take on a more disciplined and focused form. The conjunction particularly represents a great effort, where abstract notions and ideas coalesce, perhaps under the overbearing imperative of an examination or deadline. We seek answers to abstract ideas in literature and philosophy, and our overall thinking takes on a weightier tone. Thoughts become more mature and serious, as the result of an especially influential mental experience or a prolonged spell spent studying The Great Books. This may result in a more cautious and deliberate way of speaking, or our voice itself may become deeper or richer, with an impressively enlarged vocabulary.

Saturn opposition Mercury on the other hand, can be a time when clever ideas fail to live up to the constraints of a given situation. What we think is not the same as what is expected of us and we have to come to an accommodation between the two. In work situations, the political necessity to toe the party line or remain 'on message' may become quite overwhelming. This transit is the enemy of free-thinking, though a strong character can use it as an opportunity to rebel and make a statement of his own. Duty requires a man to do something he does not agree with or fully understand and he has to reconcile his obligations, or find some other way of expressing himself. The opposition is the aspect of relationship, so Mercury at its furthest point from Saturn is ironically given a fuller perspective, and our own Shadow is put under the spotlight. New insights come under the opposition, but we do not leave them as mere passing notions, but are more likely to act or comment upon them in some strong and lasting way.

If ever there was a mental block, Saturn square Mercury is it. The individual may be required to take an expedient form of action for a while, or do something he cannot explain or account for. Sometimes a formal, structured way of thinking can seem quite pointless or arbitrary, and we do not do ourselves justice by refusing to fit in with it. This may take the form of a boring course of study, or job or relationship that is not mentally stimulating. Asking questions of a broader, more philosophical nature does not seem quite appropriate: Mercury is concerned with conveying facts and specific information, not so much with idealistic notions. Deciding our own position on a given issue can also be a very creative phase, where we discover a great deal about how we really see the world.

Easy aspects between Saturn and Mercury are times when the individual can express himself clearly and easily. Study, research and putting our house in order, in the sense of important bills and paperwork, are favoured because we are both lucid about what we are doing and have a sound sense of a final outcome. These types of transit are also a gift for any writer, for they can put their meaning across, and also get good value for their efforts. Any deed or action starts as an idea, and mind over matter is truly never so obvious as at these times. We can manifest our intentions out of the air by having the right kind of focused thought. As with any helpful Saturn transit, it is worth marking these events in red in the ephemeris and putting some solid preparation in.

Style versus Substance. Saturn-Venus transits

Venus rules life's pleasures, love, luxury and fun so there is always an adjustment to Saturn's austere transiting impact. In the same way as Saturn's day follows Venus's in the week, Saturn embodies the hangover and feeling of penitence on a typical weekend lie-in. Saturn always acts as a *moderating* influence and even with the smooth transits, trine and sextile, he requires that the need for company, creativity and fun is integrated with a sense of responsibility. Hard transiting aspects here can be especially difficult because Venus governs the pleasures that round a life out, which for most people make it worth living.

Venus, therefore represents a kind of positive escapism. So

many human problems: control, dependency, desperation, can be traced back to a basic desire to avoid loneliness. For many people, no relationship is so terrible that it is not better than being on their own, which is what makes the stakes in hard Saturn-Venus transits so high. Even in a solid, durable partnership, a square or opposition from Saturn asks questions and in purely behavioural terms, we may withdraw somewhat, or else become overly anxious and needy. The challenge, as usual with Saturn, is not to manifest our fear by allowing it to spawn out of control.

Saturn conjunct Venus is a time of new beginnings where a relationship may experience a new backdrop. A heavy job or new baby for instance, may cut down the available time for fun. Or a partner is going through difficult times and we have to be extra sympathetic and supportive, which takes an eventual strain, no matter how good our intentions. If this is the first Saturn-Venus conjunction as an adult, it may be the first time a person has been in a relationship where it is impossible to simply quit and move on. Children, financial commitments, a partner requiring care, guilt, or chronic indecision may all apply pressure to keep us in the partnership. Ironically, it is this sense of being trapped that exacerbates the desire to break away and a vicious cycle ensues. Once Saturn has moved past Venus, the pressure releases and we can take a more reflective approach.

In a similar way to Saturn moving through the Seventh house, there is a strong feeling of fate to these transits. Dealings with people are different from operating with ideas or career and the workings of relationships allow us to see fate in particularly vivid terms. This idea of a fated relationship also provides a clue to ways of dealing with Saturn's energy and how to embrace his lessons.

Venus-Saturn is the absolute archetype of the mature relationship, and part of this adult attitude is realizing that relationships carry lessons and are cyclical by nature. One relationship does not work out and we leave our partner for another. Or we become unreasonable or unwilling to work at being with someone, and we are the ones who are abandoned. A certain amount of experience tells us that some people are irreplaceable in our lives and we cannot simply go out and get another model.

So Saturn ensures that the serial monogamist who runs away from a relationship will encounter the same partner over and again in different guises. Even assuming this fickle sort is always lucky enough to find somebody else, the same issues surface continually. Not exactly the same, and not to an equal extent necessarily, but familiar enough. He leaves someone because he finds them uncomfortably possessive. Then taking up with a new partner, he finds it is she who is the free spirited one and he who ends up gnawing his knuckles and issuing ultimatums. This is not a justification for staying in an unsuitable situation, still less one that is damaging or abusive, but essentially our relationships are all with an aspect of ourselves. Until we face the problem and find someone who reasonably approximates our inner psychic model, the conundrum never completely goes away. We are always running away from ourselves.

The fated quality of sharp Saturn-Venus transits in particular, also manifest in ways that are not so easy or clear-cut to define. Saturn's self-sufficient nature means that someone we have depended upon emotionally may be out of reach or appears to withdraw. This occurs particularly under the transiting square or opposition, often, perversely, just when everything seems to be going well. We have been getting on, neither side has been overly unreasonable, and in many ways this may be the high-water mark of the love affair. A karmic stress-point arrives, highlighting issues in the relationship that have not been a problem before, and we experience this as fate. One party has become bored or needs a new challenge and the partnership reaches a defining moment. This does not have to be terminal for the happy couple, but the seven-year itch is simply one of the organic periods in the nature of a relationship. A long-lasting love union may go through several of these prickly points and always finds a way to change and evolve.

A relationship that survives is not even necessarily in both party's best interests. Again, this does not mean cruel or unreasonable behaviour, but a situation where two people do not achieve more together than they would separately. The struggle to live up (or down) to a partner's expectations can be stifling to anyone's self-expression. Co-dependency is a rather clinical term, but it is a perfectly reasonable expectation if both partners share the load. Hard Saturn-Venus transits point up the conflict between work and love, and upon splitting up, people often throw themselves into their work, achieving many of the things they never managed while they were married. Ironically, they become the success as a single person that their partner always wanted them to be. Given the choice most would prefer to be still in the relationship, but this is not always an alternative.

Saturn-Venus transits may represent an age difference in a new relationship, though this depends on respective natal aspects. Anyone with a strong natal Saturn-Venus contact, either supportive or challenging, may expect at least one important relationship with someone several years older or younger. By transit, the age difference is also highly symbolic, though can either be a blessing or a crucial flaw. An older partner inevitably represents Saturn, and under smooth transits is the perfect embodiment of steadiness and calm maturity. In more stressful times, however, these same qualities become stuffy, stultifying and sum up the very nature of the problem. Saturn-Venus transits of all kinds can represent the time when we are looking for a little more maturity, or there is a reminder that time is passing and we better look to settle down. What was okay in our teens, twenties or even thirties is no longer enough and we need a little more substance and security.

Venus is also Goddess of the arts, and this may be a time to work hard on some creative plans, or our work itself takes on a more Venusian aspect. A common claim for the artist is that relationships have no downside: if things are going well, they are happy, if they are going badly, they have plenty of inspiration. Few people, surely, are crazy or manipulative enough to engineer a split simply as an invitation to their Muse, but there is an important truth buried here: Venusian qualities can be injected into life as much through the arts as by relationships, for there is romance in both. Anyone suffering during a stressful Saturn-Venus transit, feeling lonely or confused, can immerse themselves in art or creativity as a welcome and perfectly valid love substitution, or antidote to heartache[9].

Values and luxury items are both Venus matters, and hard transits here can represent a time when ease and refinement seem hard to come by. Fine clothes and expensive jewellery are not necessities perhaps, but it is preferable to deal in more than the bare essentials for anyone not aspiring to become a monk. This transit can go either way: cheaper brands may be perfectly adequate and lacking only in a superficial designer label, or after the third time having to take the shoddy stereo system back, we rue our false economy. Buy well, buy once. The Saturnian lesson seems to be to look at the essential quality of an item and not be swayed either by brand name on one hand, or a high price tag on the other.

The Sword and the Stone - Saturn-Mars transits

If Saturn is the traditional bogeyman of astrology, then Mars is his partner in crime. Rowdy, energetic, prickly, passionate, Mars is an up front planet with lots of attitude. By a strange paradox, Saturn is in his fall in Mars's sign, Aries, while Mars exalts in Capricorn, Saturn's sign. Saturn suffers in Aries because he is too rash, while Mars does well in Capricorn because he is persevering and there is an evident difference between the two. Saturn-Mars transits bring out the distinction between thoroughness and recklessness, duty and daring. At best, this combination brings an effortless strength and economy of power, where we have energy and endurance in equal measure.

This reveals a great deal about the approach necessary for hard Saturn-Mars transits. It is not essential to power ahead at break-neck speed, but to keep going regardless and show persistence. Mars is hasty and impulsive, but as long as the end goal is kept in sight and there is at least constructive progress, he is reasonably happy. The analogy is of a traffic jam. In theory the motorway is the fastest route between two points, but when the traffic backs up, it is the most frustrating experience in the world. Taking a more roundabout trip requires planning and greater concentration, but the journey may be quicker and more rewarding, as long as the end goal is kept in sight at all times. Mars likes to feel movement, but Saturn conjunct Mars is the time to refine energy and start working in a more constructive way.

Mars is a soldier and needs to be involved in a battle to be fully engaged and alive. But in aspect to Saturn, he is promoted to an officer's rank, a captain or general, planning strategy with wider responsibilities. In hard aspect, the direct route may not be appropriate; there are logistics to consider and morale has to be maintained over a long campaign. Rushing ahead blindly is pointless and no general should engage in a battle he cannot win. The general's guiding principle is also to keep the end objective in mind at all times, and certainly not to become entrenched in a war of attrition. Saturn-Mars transits often represent precisely such a stalemate or stand-off, and there are definite duties to attend to before a breakout is achieved.

It is much easier to work at a goal that seems purposeful and meaningful and is not simply a way of marking time. There is a difference between movement and action. This involves work and a general sense of progress, however it is defined, which is shown in the natal placement of Mars as the backdrop to the transit. It is important to keep the end goal in sight, but at the same time to enjoy and feel in the moment every step of the way. If the end goal becomes the be-all and end-all, then every instant that we are denied fulfilment becomes intolerable. We should think in terms of the journey not the destination; the work and not the result. It is more ideal to do something for the intrinsic joy of it than to be looking ahead in anticipation of crossing the finishing line. A steady, incremental approach to a long-range plan is far better than to fly into a rage because everything has not been achieved yesterday. Some of the thwarted sense we have under these transits may be fate, and we are mysteriously compelled to take our time, even against our will. Other times, we may be pressured by duty and deadlines and the lesson is to simply *do* a particular thing without deliberating endlessly.

The Saturn-Mars opposition is a time when we should be clear what we are doing and any superfluous effort is cut away. Never is the tug-of-war metaphor more appropriate. The house where Saturn is transiting is often the biggest source of frustration, though the opposition represents two halves of a complete whole. If frustration overwhelms, it is always as well to have plenty to do, and weights, training shoes or a punch-bag are excellent investments. Working and applying steady effort cannot help but further our long term aims, and makes the final breakthrough more satisfying when it inevitably happens. However, after say, the first agonisingly slow retrograde of transiting Saturn to Mars, this can be a time when we kick doors, grind our teeth, and anything close enough to hand gets flung across the room.

Fear with any other planet results in shrinking, withdrawal and reticence, but Mars is not like this. Mars hits out, does battle and asserts himself, and under the Saturn opposition especially, is always more likely to 'get his retaliation in first'. Violence is always a possibility here, especially if there is a deep anger that has remained bottled up and unexpressed. In this case, accidents or strong animosity may come to us from the outside, and it may be worth an honest look in the mirror to see how, if at all, this has come about. In personal relationships, our partners suffer the consequences of us projecting our frustration outwards, with the partner being viewed as a problem or obstacle. We see everything as someone else's fault. There may be a standoff situation, with egos heavily involved, and any reconciliation tends to be viewed in terms of a climb-down or losing face. Sex is a Mars issue that is often best for working out such frustrations.

For both men and women, sexual problems may also manifest under Saturn-Mars transits, usually as a symptom of something deeper in the relationship being amiss. In many ways, these two planets represent the paradox of the irresistible force and the immovable object, so a purely material approach usually results in a standoff or stalemate. This combination manifests in all sorts of colourful ways in the bedroom, but far from a block or hindrance, the individual's may receive some important insights in his own attitude to sex. There are psychological issues here and treating sex as a purely mechanical act is usually part of the problem. The Saturn-Mars opposition especially make the individual realise there are subtler ways of working than sheer brute force. Inasmuch as Mars represents assertion and dominance, the opposite of this is submission and compliance. The familiar frustration and delay of Saturn may be sublimated in a more positive way, as deliberation and surrender, force and submission are integrating into lovemaking.

Stick or Twist - Saturn-Jupiter transits

Saturn's transits to Jupiter do not feel as intimate, nor immediate as those to the inner planets, but influence the individual's wider issues and beliefs. Jupiter is about faith and the law, a sense of fair play and one's personal philosophy. Jupiter is the opposite of Saturn: the Greater Benefic, where instead of fear and contraction, there is confidence and expansion. Saturn is a chasm, Jupiter a bridge. Jupiter represents belief, confidence and a kind of bumptious optimism: all the things that Saturn struggles with. A test of faith often arises under the hard transits, where a comforting Jupiterian philosophy comes up against the Saturnian real-world experience.

By transit, Saturn moulds Jupiter's basic desire to inflate and focuses it in a realistic and practical way. By conjunction, Saturn may initially constrict Jupiter, providing a kind of straightjacket, or at least some positive structure to his natural desire to expand. Instead of natural confidence, there may be an excessive preoccupation with the proper thing, knowing our place, not getting above ourselves. If we wish to be rich or famous, then we have to work hard and earn it. The desire to grow and enlarge our world may be taken down the 'correct channels' with Saturn transits inclining us towards the conventional route in any situation: becoming rubber stamped, and properly professional.

Saturn-Jupiter transits also represent an accommodation with the real world in economic terms. Jupiter is the ruler of wealth, and his insouciant attitude is to be infinitely generous and open handed towards everyone: buy now, pay later and tomorrow never comes. Saturn is a bean counter, who wants to save for the inevitable rainy day and have everything accounted for on spreadsheets, with all invoices and receipts. Taken to extremes, this may describe a kind of genteel poverty, and someone who is, temporarily at least, all status and no money. Deciding how much is enough becomes a big question between these two influences and there is a middle way to be found between the excesses of boom and bust. At best, a well-handled fusion of Jupiter's confidence and Saturn's competence offers enormous potential and we may anticipate steady and prudent growth under the influence of a Saturn-Jupiter trine or sextile.

Time and Tide - *Saturn-Saturn transits*

Saturn represents time itself, so his orbit is the chief timekeeper, the marker of life's staging posts and rites of passage. Saturn's aspects to himself are all fundamental building blocks of time, occurring at precise points of course, but the hard transiting seven-year cycle seems to herald best of all important ages, or significant points in life. The Saturn Return is the best known and probably most crucial stage, but Saturn's aspects to itself all carry weight.

Young people especially are taken by surprise by Saturn reaching a point where life seems to alter quite radically and for no apparent reason. Once again, Saturnian rites of passage represent organic change. The first Saturn-Saturn square at aged seven represents the formative period of life. This is early childhood and the impressionable shaping period of the psyche. Fourteen is the first Saturn opposition, where adolescence kicks in. No wonder this is such a difficult age, where teenagers start physically maturing and seeing themselves as separate from their law-giving parents. The opposition is frequently a point of rebellion, where confused or angry youngsters experience a sense of separation; questioning what they have done up to this point, and what they have been forced to accept.

Even people in their twenties do not yet have the experience to know that their present passage of life is not necessarily the shape of the future, but merely a passing phase. The transition from age nineteen to twenty for instance does not appear so significant as from twenty to twenty-one. Twenty-one, or three quarters of a

Saturn cycle, is a very significant point, though for reasons that are inscrutable. Why this particular transits should carry so much weight is uncertain, but the last applying square to Saturn brings a noticeable change of perspective in many ways more obviously than the Saturn return itself. Not for nothing is this age referred to as the 'key of the door'. The young person crosses this threshold and becomes quite well adjusted to life in his twenties, until the Saturn return comes along and raises the bar once more. This syndrome is not restricted solely to young people, of course: throughout life, we go through successive Saturnian compartments, with the path ahead progressively narrowing down.

The Big Two Nine and a Half

Between its sign and house placement, Saturn offers an opportunity for excellence. This is especially so through the fabled Saturn Return: the doorway to astrological adulthood. The first Saturn return at aged twenty-nine is the culmination of our first in-depth experience of all the zodiacal houses, and the second Saturn return is a further refinement and mature completion. Well handled, the first Return should ensure a smooth progression into the next thirty- year passage: if not, then many important lessons and adjustments have to come in the approach to age fifty-eight. Not a great deal of information exists on people's experiences of their *third* Saturn return, but suffice it to say by this point the maturing process should be well underway[10].

Saturn's return refers strictly to his exact natal degree, but may fairly be said to represent the entire transit of Saturn's natal house. In fact there are three components: the natal degree, the natal sign, and the natal house, all of which are part of the experience.

Commonsense is required, for depending on the size of the house, the Saturn return experience may last for anything up to five years, but certainly the issues that are examined may be felt for at least a year either side of the exact conjunction. Not so much an event, as a process, and as the lessons may remain with us for life, it is not easy to determine a precise cut-off point.

So often spoken of as a dark and scary time when the bottom inevitably drops out of a person's life, the extent to which the first Saturn Return is difficult depends on how far the individual has faced up to the particular challenge of the sign and house of his Saturn. Seven, thirteen-to-fourteen and twenty-one are all landmark ages that bring noticeable changes in psychological perspective, and the next rite of passage is probably thought of as reaching thirty. Not quite, however: thirty *itself* is perhaps not as important or stressful as aged twenty eight to nine; an age which does not receive much attention outside of astrological circles, but is a critical step in growing into adult consciousness. The Big Two Nine And A Half gives a double dose of whatever Saturn represents in the natal chart as he begins to reach his full potential. Dreams of all sorts may come up against reality with an uncomfortable bump at this time and it is only the practical and viable options that survive.

How far we have lived or avoided living out Saturn may depend on its natal condition: there is a greater temptation to sidestep a difficult Saturn with hard aspects than one that flows easily and accepts the need for work. Equally, however, an afflicted or overbearing Saturn can be very *hard* to ignore and in such cases, people who have been compelled to toil under difficult conditions over several years find life growing steadily more rewarding once they are through the twenty-nine year doorway. How exacting the Saturn Return is depends on how far we have lived life on our own terms, or else tried to fit in with another person's life template. Attempting to shoehorn our way through the wrong Saturn portal is a mistake, but most people actually do not mind working hard at something they enjoy, so the main cause for concern is *getting on the right road.*

The image is of trying to get into a party or club, which has a large and intimidating bouncer at the door, who strangely enough, is dressed in a hood and wields a sickle. If we are comfortable and have the appropriate invitation or back stage laminate, then we are left alone to enjoy our evening and to access all areas. However, if a man bluffs his way in without the proper pass, or pretends to be someone else, then there is a constant feeling of unease. He tries to mix and make conversation but there is a sense that he does not fit in, and besides, the hooded bouncer's eyes are beaming a hole in his back all night, until at last he feels compelled to leave and only feels fit to come back once he has the right credentials.

Going for the path in life we truly want requires courage, however, especially if the goal appears to go against the grain of convention. Saturn is convention personified, of course, so it is somewhat in the nature of the Saturn return to reconcile our own fundamental truth with the pressures and formal expectations of our environment. Parents, spouses, bosses or authority figures may picture us in different terms than we see ourselves, but we cannot be overly swayed by other people's views. We should know our own business best. From the relative ease and freedom of the twenties, the need for concrete choice takes on a greater imperative.

It sometimes appears to our secret, pessimistic Saturnian self that life would be easier if we were all accountants or administrators steadily working thirty-five hours a week at a government office and putting something away for our retirement. This scenario suits many people very well of course, but it does not hold out much hope for anyone wishing for a more adventurous career: an artist, acrobat or astrologer. Giving way to a distorted Shadow image, having a sensible haircut and getting a 'proper job', by way of abandoning our real truth is a bad use of Saturn energy. This is an expedient measure at best, and only means that we will be forever haunted by the siren song of our true Saturn calling somewhere in the distance. What Saturn really demands is that we apply his qualities of hard work, discipline and persistence to whatever our vocation happens to be. Very often, working in an ambitious or unconventional occupation requires much *greater* effort and discipline, because there are fewer people available to do the work and the support structures do not exist.

In fact, one of the great boons post-Saturn return is an appreciation that we can be pretty much whatever we want, if we are prepared to work at it. With good health and a reasonably sound mind, and given our generally greater confidence and experience, we can do everything in our thirties that we could in the twenties, and probably slightly better. The mystique that certain professions or positions hold when we are younger starts to evaporate as we realise that doctors, policemen, politicians and pop stars are just like anyone else. They have made their decisions and sacrifices and though we may not like to take the same risks, there is equally no special status awarded for putting safety first. The Saturn return highlights the balance between having some solid measure of achievement, against relying excessively on superficial success badges: steady job, acceptable salary, foreign holidays and a house in the right postal district. It becomes a reward in itself to become successful at something we are good at.

Most people find the need for at least some adjustment at the Saturn return, however, and these can seem daunting. Going from the experiments of the twenties into the more settled business of the thirties is a rite of passage not formally recognised. It's a hurdle – the time when we are not just satisfied to hold our own, but there is a prompting to stretch further, push the boundaries and have a little more. After twenty eight-to-nine, the feeling should be that we are no longer at the crossroads with forks leading off in all directions, but like tributaries of a great river, the streams come together as they approach the sea. After this, we know who we are and what we do. Choices become finite and seemingly more irrevocable – making life-defining decisions with further-reaching consequences represents another of the main differences in being past thirty. Again, if we have followed an appropriate course, this narrowing down of life may be welcomed – we just become more focused and specialised at what we are good at and enjoy. But if, to use a rather dramatic term, we have been living a lie, then it becomes steadily harder to bluff it out; it is a much more involved process to turn things around until the agonising reappraisal becomes more and more inevitable.

The Saturn Return is an organic point where physical ageing becomes more noticeable for many people, with grey hairs for example often making their first sobering appearance in the late twenties. Astrologer Stephen Arroyo[11] has pointed out that our bodily centre of gravity shifts downward after the Saturn Return, from the neck region toward the abdomen and pelvis. Certainly, it may become more of an effort to keep in shape, as our metabolism slows down and the first signs of bodily filling out, or a middle aged spread start to appear. Biological imperatives; the women's body clock for instance, may start to kick in later now, but the countdown probably still begins in earnest once through Saturn's portal. Parenthood is a momentous enough event in itself, but the various sacrifices and shifts in priority that it brings are given extra material significance when it coincides with Saturn's return.

The second Saturn return is clearly in a different context, and rather than seeing the issues as those which will shape an adult life, there is a stronger feeling of completion. At twenty-nine, some goals drop away because they are not fulfilling or appropriate. At fifty-eight, there is a sense that some ambitions have to be reconciled because there is not enough time to see them through. Saturn's gateway narrows down and if any new paths are begun, they must be things that can be achieved in the remaining years. Still, this is the defining point in many people's lives, especially those in positions of social influence or high office. The late fifties are a politician or businessman's prime years, when he reaches his peak of working maturity. For a public figure of long-standing, the second Saturn return is also a big determining factor on his legacy and how he will be remembered.

For outwardly less ambitious sorts, the second Saturn return may be a positive liberation. The children are grown up and the mortgage paid, as retirement approaches. Rather than building a life up, in the sense of the first Return, there should be more emphasis on easing down and reducing commitments. It becomes a time to enjoy the things that there was never time to explore before with so many worldly Saturnian obligations. There is a more inward orientation, leisure becomes far more important and instead of ambition, the Saturnian emphasis is on stripping down and simplifying. By this point, the mature individual knows what he wants and more importantly what he does not want, and deals as far as possible only with the essentials.

After the first Saturn return, the age of thirty-six is the next seven year staging point. Vedic authorities state that this is the age where Saturn comes to its full strength and power. It takes this long for us really to understand Saturn, though our understanding may still yet be in the initial stages. By the mid-thirties, the sign qualities of natal Saturn should at least not appear so intimidating and we can relax into a more stable and conservative role. This is commonly the age when a generation starts to climb the ladder of corporate and political power and to assume greater societal responsibility.

Forty-two- to- three is the next seven-year stage, the second Saturn-Saturn opposition. This is the first real test of the direction we took at the Saturn return, some fourteen years previously. If we chose wisely at that point, we may find increasing fulfilment and a sense of reaping a harvest: life indeed be said to begin at forty three. There are sure to be some questions, however, where the approaching 'change' occurs, for women certainly, and possibly for men too. Though the biological clock ticks down more slowly in the 21st Century, by this Saturn-Saturn opposition point, the issue of children becomes steadily more finite. It is not too late to start or to enlarge a family, but it probably represents the last chance. The existence of an actual male menopause is debatable, but the Saturn-Saturn opposition for men has many of the same archetypal concerns. Anything that has not worked out from the Saturn return onward cannot be maintained and it is time for some serious life surgery. Not every middle-aged man will necessarily buy a sports car and run off with a stripper, but this point (so soon after the Uranus half-return), may signify a major reorientation.

Forty-nine to fifty is equally as important for most people. Regardless that we are living longer now, fifty is sometimes reported as among the most difficult ages, when the transition from being middle aged to being more senior takes place. Unless the individual accepts that they are older and more mature and finds a job or relationship that reflects this, they may be in for testing times. This applies especially if they wish to make a new start. Yet fifty may also be regarded as a working person's prime, where they have energy as well as influence, and their peak of achievement approaches. High office and the corridors of power are conspicuously full of people in their sixth decade. This is the three quarter point of the second Saturn cycle - in effect, it is the Saturn return of aged twenty-one. Once again, this point has an unusual, though quite palpable quality all of its own, no matter how many times it is lived through.

Easy aspects between Saturn and itself are less dramatic than the squares and oppositions, but still have an archetypal quality. Saturn-Saturn trines come approximately every nine and a half years, and these are like harvests or pit-stops on a race. Eighteen is the common age of majority, while after the Saturn return, the late thirties are once again an age when many people start taking on more influential roles in work, family and government. We are rewarded for hard work and start to enjoy a pleasing maturity. The resistance of the hard aspects no longer presses down and there is greater potential for self-determination. Rather than try to force or manoeuvre a way into a position of authority, success comes more spontaneously. We can do things because we choose to, rather than because we have to.

Inspiration versus Perspiration - *Saturn-Uranus transits*

Saturn and Uranus have strong mythological connections and their mutual link in the sign rulership of Aquarius suggests some of the issues that arise under their transits. Uranus was Saturn's father in mythology, whom Chronos overthrew, before he was toppled by his own son, Jupiter. If Saturn is convention and formality, then Uranus is freedom, rebellion and originality. Transits between these two planets always bring a trade-off or accommodation between the established paths against a freer, more anarchic spirit: roundheads versus cavaliers. Hard Saturn-Uranus transits signify the need for a revolution, and relationships, enterprises and occupations that have become redundant and oppressive are symbolically taken to the guillotine.

Saturn conjunct Uranus signifies the time when we can inject the Uranian originality into life, applying it practically, rather than simply constructing castles in the air. Though Saturn begins as a somewhat stifling influence, in fact he channels Uranus in such a way as he becomes more viable and workable. A more innovative solution to a long-standing problem may arise and instead of simply talking about it or demonstrating it on paper, we take steps and deliver results. A normal-formal Saturn situation at work that has become mere empty procedure has new life injected into it, or else disappears under the impact of an abrupt Uranian lighting bolt. A successful blend of these two planet's energies comes more often under the transiting trine, but wherever they meet there is potential for a new twist on an old idea.

By opposition or square, Saturn lays down a challenge to the wilder and freer means of expression favoured by Uranus, and always seems to present problems and practical difficulties to the whimsical attitude. So instead of working freelance in some cutting-edge technological field, the individual has to conform for a while to a middling position that pays the mortgage and gets him credentials for the future. Only afterwards can he become the innovative genius or entrepreneur of his imaginings. Or in relationship terms, instead of an experimental liaison with an exotic, pan-sexual partner, a man comes home of an evening to settle down on the sofa and watch television with someone who provides a sense of security.

Transits to Uranus are a generational experience, which brings in a peer pressure of sorts; a kind of yardstick by which we measure our success, values and happiness. We may feel somewhat out on a limb by embracing more individual or alternative paths, while those who have grown up alongside us are having families or rising up the corporate ladder. Everyone makes their choices, of course, and no two people's priorities are the same. Those with great worldly commitments may envy the freedom of someone who has taken a determinedly unconventional course. There is a positive reading to the Saturn reality check if the individual reins back some of his more outré ideas and achieves a little perspective. It is one thing to be individual and uncompromising, but not at the risk of becoming a rebel without a cause.

The Devil and the Deep Blue Sea - *Saturn-Neptune transits*
Possibly no two planets are more different in behaviour and attributes than Saturn and Neptune. Saturn is the material world and Neptune is the Otherworld; so here we have a combination of the material and divine, and their transiting aspects carry the suggestion of all or nothing[12]. It is in the nature of Neptune to be subtle, or downright slippery, and rather than announcing itself with obvious fanfare (like some other planets we know), both when transiting and being transit*ed*, it rather sneaks up and whispers in our ear. Unless we are inveterate ephemeris watchers, we may not even realise we are *having* a Neptune transit until after the event, or at least not until the transit is well underway. Furthermore, Neptune's boundless, all-pervasive quality means we are apt to mistake its effects for a more generalised feeling of despondency, euphoria or whatever. But while it is not always easy to pinpoint *specifics* with Neptune, we are left with no doubt that something quite profound has happened.

In hard aspect, these two planets signify a fundamental dissonance and inability to reconcile dreams and aspirations with the imperatives of everyday life. Divine discontent is too mild a description for the feeling of physical matter bearing down and there appearing to be no pattern or poetry in the world. Spiritual sculptures or images remain stone and we lack the faith that our precious beliefs carry any weight, or our prayers are heard in any higher sphere. Particularly with the opposition, the Saturn-Neptune brings a miasma of melancholy and disenchantment, or if supported by natal aspects, a more profound feeling of depression, stemming from a kind of cosmic letdown or pathos.

It may also lead to a desire for oblivion in drink, drugs or whatever we use to blur the edges of the day. This can be quite a distressing feeling, and there is a weakness for putting the worst possible perspective on any given situation. Any big decision made at the Saturn-Neptune opposition takes on the proportions of a doomed, romantic sacrifice and we dramatise our distress in ways that would not disgrace a Gothic novel. It appears as if we have fallen out of heaven, though the bump brought about by impacting Saturn is probably the exact kind of wakeup call that we need. We can lie to ourselves under a Neptunian influence for as long as we wish to hold on to a gaudy, kaleidoscopic impression of the world. But after adjusting to a slightly cooler and more starkly-toned environment, we realise that the illusory world we had occupied had become untenable and probably harmful, and a larger scale reorientation is in order. The hangover period or detoxification is not quite appreciated until after the event.

Supportive transits from Saturn to Neptune on the other hand are among the most profoundly mystical and rewarding of all, when the grinding Saturnian gears appear to be in temporary suspension. The transiting sextile, and more especially the trine, are times when we can make dreams come true and a prolonged period of wishing comes to a more miraculous fulfilment than could possibly be designed or contrived. Here the material and spiritual are in perfect accord and it is possible to pluck a job, love, money, home or whatever, as if out of the ether. There is an element of fantasy to this kind of event and the inevitable moral, without which no fable or fairytale is complete, revolves around maintaining our faith. Goals are accomplished not by feats of strength, endurance, or ambition, but by a kind of grace. Plan ahead for these transits and dream large when they are impending.

As Above, So Below - *Saturn-Pluto transits*

Each of the outer planets can be considered malefic in its own way; the anarchic perversity of Uranus or the nebulous uncertainty of Neptune. Pluto, however, is a different proposition altogether. Pluto represents a trip into the underworld, a sometimes hellish journey that brings us back up into the world more aware of the deeper and darker side of life. There is a maniacal intensity and desire for mastery connected with Pluto, an obsessive need to understand and control. This is very much like Saturn of course, except Saturn is very much of the present world, rather than any other dimension. Saturn is earthly aging and death, Pluto is what we may face on the other side. Pluto represents power as well: material, egotistic power, plutocrats and underworld figures, with a ruthless streak and who do not mind what they do or who they upset.

By transit, therefore, Saturn regulates the individual's use of power, and in a positive way makes it operate in a more structured and disciplined way. Still, the propensity to act out of fear is very great and these transits may be where we hit out at other people, or imagine that they are trying to undermine or get at us. The conjunction of Saturn and Pluto is where we may start on a new regime or attitude. We need to effect a transformation, represented by the house natal Pluto occupies and that Saturn transits. We channel our power in a purposeful direction and any extraneous elements that have outlived their usefulness, are toast. There may be a great fear of letting go as we become suddenly aware of the intense power of Pluto and his ability to transform us utterly.

Pluto represents visceral, deep down issues; taboo or secret matters and things not mentioned in polite conversation. Saturn has its usual effect of giving solidity and reality to a thing, and this can represent a time when such Plutonian affairs come to the fore: disease, power, manipulation, revenge; all of the things that go on underneath the surface of life but are rarely addressed openly, or even acknowledged.

For very young people, Saturn-Pluto transits may the first eye-opening encounter with the uglier physical and emotional side of sex; the overwhelming sensations aroused through lust and jealousy. No matter what our age, or how sophisticated we believe ourselves to be, these transits can be a loss of innocence.

As usual, the square of Saturn is the point where it becomes hard to reconcile or integrate the transited planet's affairs. With Pluto, there is a conflict between the need to control and cling on, versus the need to eliminate and let go. A radical clear-out of our possessions can be quite liberating, especially with the easier transits, and a small industry has grown up around the cult of space clearing and Feng-Shui. Alternatively, daily work may become quite Plutonian, taking in anything from plumbing, to recycling, scholarly research or depth psychology.

Saturn transiting the Nodes

In a culture that does not uniformly accept reincarnation, the intrinsic meaning of the Nodes as signposts of a life has become somewhat diluted. Both Saturn and the Nodes have especial karmic significance: Saturn in terms of work and specific lessons, the Nodes in terms of overall direction or orientation. The house of the North Node especially is critical, and the more an individual gets into this area, the happier generally he will be. Like Saturn moving across the natal ascendant, his transit of the North Node represents a defining moment. Either by fate or design, or a combination of the two, this is the start of a significant new direction that continues for the next eighteen years. Rather like the eclipses that the Nodes signify, events at either point do not *appear* particularly momentous necessarily, but are appreciated more in retrospect. Like a karmic New Moon, it is probably the beginning of a complete cycle of activity. This involves work of course, but the North Node is about conscious activity, and shows the area where our own efforts are used to bring something about. It may appear that a transition is made without any apparent effort on our behalf, and like a new Act in a play or drama, a different backdrop to our activities is spontaneously created.

Saturn's conjunction to the South Node is similar, except it is more like something which is out of our own hands. It has somewhat of a negative connotation, in that we *react*, rather than act. Instead of a positive opportunity being presented, something appears to be taken away which forces us to make a life adjustment. This may itself be positive and liberating, and once again, there is an overwhelming sense of a big moment having arrived.

CHAPTER FIVE

WHAT'S YOUR PROBLEM?

Saturn Transiting the Houses

Try this experiment: talk to a friend you haven't seen for a while and from your conversation, make a mental note of where their main problem seems to be. Job? Relationship? Home? Money? Kids? Check out your friend's horoscope afterwards, and whatever house Saturn is transiting, the chances are the issues of that house are the source of their complaint. A perverse game, perhaps, but it rarely fails[13].

The house that Saturn is transiting is where anybody's main lessons and focus of attention lies at any given time. When Saturn goes through a house, he gives a thorough grounding in its issues, a complete immersion and master-class, so the matter is understood vividly through having been *lived*. Saturn's stay brings tests and trials that we can pass, but only with more effort than we thought necessary at the outset, and with definite more or less pre-ordained experiences along the way. This is not to say that he causes suffering necessarily: the fated experience may be quite positive and liberating, depending on the birth chart and the individual's consciousness. Fate manifests on many levels, but understanding what Saturn is trying to teach is an essential first step.

Saturn demands that the affairs of a given domain are made solid and concrete, and we *build* wherever he is placed. Structures are set up to shelter us from the sense of a Void, or universal emptiness that Saturn creates. Such cosmic darkness cannot easily be materially filled or satisfied, and the balance to strike is between a viable structure and inner, spiritual worth. Saturn exalts in the sign of balance, and jobs, relationships, homes and creative enterprises that provide grounding and security should stand up perfectly well, as long as we do not *overly* depend on them. Some things are made solid that we wish were not – fears manifest themselves, hard work becomes inevitable, ghosts from the past materialize, trials, frustrations and annoyances are made real and actual. Anything failing the test of manifestation probably passes out of a life, maybe with a sense of failure, or else possibly, of welcome release.

Saturn's two and a half year stay in each sign is perfectly adequate for his lessons to be absorbed; indeed his tenure at certain tricky points can seem endless. He is slow moving of course, but it is more that he is such an *un-ignorable* planet whose effects cannot be marginalised or put on hold. Compared to the relative stasis of the outer planets, however, there is still a feeling of movement and progression: a noticeable arc of development through a sign that can be evaluated as a whole while it is lived. So much does Saturn test and stretch us that we may carry a deep aversion to the affairs of a house for a long time afterwards, and like a school or university exam crammed for every night, the material has seeped into our marrow, we know it backwards and we have had *enough*. This often entails a reaction *against* the affairs of a given house after Saturn has completed his transit. For example, after an immersion in the Tenth house domain of career ambition, somebody may decide to quit the corporate hamster wheel and downshift to the country. They then get into more group-oriented and idealistic work as symbolised by the Eleventh house. Or after a Saturn in the Fourth episode, realise that they have had enough of maintaining six investment homes, sell up, and use the money to gamble or work on something creative, as represented by the Fifth house.

So the houses cannot be looked at in isolation. The issues of one house follow on from the details of the last and set the tone for the experience of the upcoming domain. So, for example, Eighth-house transits cannot be looked at in isolation from the Seventh – attitudes to sex and sharing obviously follow on from experiences of relationship, and likewise the Ninth is often a reaction to the Eighth – some grounding in philosophy may be sought after undergoing bereavement or perhaps a profound psychic or near death experience. Then, once our mental horizons have been suitably broadened by the Ninth, we want to apply our learning to something practical, like a career, which is when Saturn crosses the Mid-heaven.

Saturn's conjunction to a house *cusp* - and not just one of the angles - is often as significant as a major aspect to a personal planet. The point at which Saturn crosses a house cusp is usually the most intensive and high-stress moment of the whole passage, with the effects gradually settling down as he moves through the house. It is as if Saturn comes bursting through the door, bringing with him a dramatic gust of wind that sends everything flying, and though the portal shuts afterwards, we are left with a stern and shadowy houseguest for a while. This is an important point: Saturn's transit through a house begins as a kind of crisis, or at least our minds are focused very clearly on the matters of that area. But the whole transit is rarely if ever so severe and exhausting as the initial three to six months.

Saturn retrograding over a house cusp is like getting a second chance at a particular thing, or else there is unfinished business in the affairs of a given house. Structures made during the initial pass of Saturn through the house are not necessarily *unmade* at the first retrograde motion, but only after the final direct transit do we decide if they either pass or fail the test. Once again, the house cusps are highly sensitive points and if Saturn passes out of a house and then retrogrades back in, we are thrown back into a state of mind or action that we thought had been left behind. It is truly as if a switch has been thrown. The feelings that come up under the retrograde motion may be equally as intense as the initial transit, if not more so. More often, however, we have some recent experience to guide us and we are a little cuter the second time around.

The natal house position of Saturn provides the background context of the transit. For example, if Saturn is transiting the Tenth and natal Saturn is in the Ninth house, a job offer may come from abroad. Or if in the same example, Saturn transits the Twelfth house, then we may be imprisoned in a foreign jail (stand up, Paul McCartney). The performer with Saturn in the Fifth reflects all his Saturn transits through his art. The planetary *ruler* of a house may also be affected by Saturn's transit through its domain. So if Taurus or Libra, for example, are on the cusp or intercepted in a given house, then Saturn's transit may affect Venus issues: relationships and money. Cancer on a house cusp means the transit becomes a particularly lunar experience, affecting our emotions and sense of security. Saturn itself ruling a house cusp means events during that transit feel especially fated. And so on. Every point on the chart affects every other point, though discretion is needed as usual, for the effect can become increasingly subtle, depending on the individual chart[14]. A butterfly flapping its wings in the Tenth house does not necessarily cause an avalanche in the Fourth. It has become the norm not to describe the houses in any strict judgemental sense, and the idea of any one domain being essentially malefic has faded. But to take a more objective Saturnian stance, the issues of the Sixth, Eighth and Twelfth houses are traditionally the most demanding, dealing with work and service, sex and death, and sacrifice and hidden enemies respectively. This is not to say that these transits cannot be rewarding; if tackled head-on, they contain the most potential for positive liberation. But even in a strong and well-dignified condition, they seem to entail an especial amount of karmic heavy lifting. Conversely, the Ninth and Eleventh house are traditionally considered 'good' houses, and Saturn may be felt here with less trouble.

Saturn transiting the First House *Defining Moments.*

This transit is like a rebirth. We emerge at the gates of the first house, blinking in the sunlight, like a prisoner on release day. Coming out of the primeval swamp of the Twelfth House, we feel quite transformed, as if having taken a detour through hyperspace and landed in a different dimension. The people and places are same, but we look at them through new eyes. There is a palpable feeling of liberation and a debt expunged perhaps, but like the freed convict, the rest of our life stretches ahead and we realise we now need to pull everything together and make a proper go of it.

We appear to others more serious, assertive and purposeful after the travails of the Twelfth house, though at the same time lighter, like we have shed many burdens. The depressive introspection that characterised so much of Saturn's passage of the Twelfth lifts and the overburdening issues of that house are forgotten - forgotten completely, that is, to the extent that it may be hard to remember exactly what the problems were in the first place. Though we are still very much wrapped up in ourselves, there is a far greater imperative to be actively involved in the world.

The ascendant represents the horizon, the mystical meeting of heaven and earth, which defines the personality to such a great extent, and Saturn is what gives it solidity and reality. So, Saturn crossing the ascendant is a defining moment, when the aggregate of all the houses and all our experience to date comes together. Impressions that have formed in the months or years leading up to this point become crystallised and a man is galvanised into action. This is often a time when a momentous new course is embarked upon: starting a family, a business, or setting up home in a different country; in any case, a project that will define significantly the next circuit of Saturn around the houses.

As we become more self-conscious, our physical appearance also undergoes a change, either natural or contrived. Good news for anyone wishing to slim down is that physical weight tends to drop off by itself at this time and we may even end up looking quite fashionably lean or emaciated. Some people may start wearing glasses, with dark glasses ('shades') in particular being a distinctively Saturnian image. Others go further and have cosmetic or reconstructive surgery. A man may grow a beard and develop a taste for understated tailoring, while both men and women often decide that greying temples lend them a distinguished air. One way or the other, our clothes and demeanour take on a more mature appearance.

Saturn here is at the most strictly personal point in the horoscope, and this may have a converse effect on marriage or relationships. People are so furiously absorbed in their own affairs that their partners tend to be sidelined or neglected. If there has been any nagging sense of dissatisfaction or disquiet with a lover, friend or relation, then matters are steadily brought to a head. While we may have been somewhat passive or withdrawn as Saturn transited the Twelfth house, once out in the sunlight of the ascendant, we feel more able to speak up and be assertive. Suddenly sensitive to people's quirks, their disagreeable attitudes appear magnified, often in one little cameo performance that encapsulates everything that is annoying about them. There then comes a critical point where we decide we cannot put up with the situation any longer. Relationships of all kinds that have survived on shaky ground may fall off altogether at this point.

Arnold Schwarzenegger proved his versatility once and for all by being elected Governor of California in October 2003. As Saturn approached his Ascendant-Mercury conjunction, the former bodybuilder and movie star traded in his swimming trunks for a power suit on the way to becoming the embodiment of every immigrant's American dream. Only the fact of his Austrian parentage prevented him following in previous California Governor Ronald Reagan's path from Hollywood to the White House.

Novelist **Salman Rushdie** lived for nine years under a death sentence imposed by Muslim extremists for his 1989 book *The Satanic Verses*. The *fatwa* was officially lifted in September 1998, shortly after Saturn moved out of the darkness of his Twelfth house and hit his ascendant.

Mick Jagger became *Sir* Mick as Saturn crossed his ascendant in 2002. Always keen to be seen in the highest social circles, there never seemed any danger that he would refuse the incongruous honour.

Saturn transiting the Second House

'Money is better than poverty, if only for financial reasons'. Woody Allen.

As Saturn moves towards the second-house cusp, we get some intimation of the impending issues and it could be that we need a small fire lit underneath us to get things underway. In many ways, this is the final coming down to earth of a period that first began when Saturn entered the Twelfth house - in some charts perhaps five or six years previously. Dealing with mundane, money-making issues can be a welcome relief after the more abstract, psychologically oriented matter of the Twelfth and to a lesser extent the ascendant and the First house. People at this time are no longer so furiously self-absorbed and introspective, but start looking outside and think about getting on again in the everyday world.

Saturn has been described as the 'bank-statement planet', and during his tour through the financial zone it is easy to see why. On the face of it, this transit does not require much interpretation. Saturn moving through the Second house requires that we work on our money. How do we get it, what we do with it, and how do we feel once we have it. There are lessons here of cost versus value, how much money we need to feel secure, and to what lengths are we prepared go in order to accumulate it. Even usually non-materialistic types may feel a greater anxiety about money, which is best used as an incentive to create greater security. This could take the form of a small rainy day fund, or really discovering how to build up a money structure, in terms of savings or property. A business or enterprise started when Saturn crossed the ascendant hits its first practical tests under this transit, and the imperative is to set it up on a more secure financial footing. An aversion to vulgar luxury is not an excuse to be naïve around financial matters, and even the most ascetic type owes it to himself to get the best possible mileage from his resources.

The common-sense fear upon seeing this transit impending obviously has to do with poverty or financial privation, which can in fact be a very pressing issue, but only one side of the coin - pun intended. Most people derive their income from salaried employment, but unlike the Sixth or Tenth houses, the Second house need not directly affect *our job or work as such*. There is no reason why a pay-the-rent position at least should not be available to help us get over a temporary financial hurdle. This transit tends to affect long-term security, assets, equity and investments, rather than weekly pay or party money. If our self-esteem is unduly affected by climbing off our professional pedestal, however, and we are unwilling to adjust and find work where it becomes available, then the pressure starts to squeeze. Saturn in the second house hits hardest if we believe we are what we earn.

Circumstances under this transit are more likely to give a prod towards deciding what to do with money once we actually have some of it. Saturn's prods tend to be rather hard and sharp, of course, so if the last few years have been spent in a more contemplative, introspective phase, then a man will definitely be looking to his laurels. If there is something going on that makes working difficult – redundancy, recession, debt, looking after children, taking a course of education, then this position may cause some sleepless nights. There is a feeling of uncertainty even in an apparently secure situation, with a rather irrational fear that money may simply vanish. Every tiny purchase is examined as if we are to be mortgaged to it for years, with the constant question: 'Do I really need this thing?' The big picture may be healthy and positive, but an enforced austerity program in the immediate term provides the focus for a complete material transformation.

This is the factual backdrop of Saturn's second house transit, but as usual it is the inner attitude, in this case our values, that are most affected. After accepting the need to offload mere material encumbrances, we nobly agree to downsize or defer gratification while we work on longer-term plans, or avenues that bring greater spiritual growth. No matter what we may like to believe, our relationship with friends, family and colleagues is affected by this change in material status, especially given the kind of society we live in. We go from dressing well and getting the drinks in every night, to counting every penny until the end of the month, watching with mixed emotions while those around us carry on living it large. Snobbery often rears up under this transit and we have to deal with people who have more or less than us, and our feelings towards them.

Hoarding and collecting items, or surrounding ourselves with material goods to derive a sense of security both come under Saturn's Second House spotlight. A change of heart or a desire for greater freedom may compel us to sell up and have more space in our lives. Or, we may simply need the money and have to realise on our assets to meet expenses. While some people are lucky enough to have savings, a second home, or antiques in the attic to sell, it cuts deep to let go of the sentiment invested in these precious items, not to mention the sense of security holding on to them provides. Any sense of purely material security comes under scrutiny, so this could be something as mundane as a precious new car getting its first serious dent or unsightly scratch in its paintwork. Endowing shiny toys with too much status or sentiment is sure-fire way to heartbreak when they go the way of all flesh.

Shopping and spending money tie in with ancient human hunter-gathering instincts. We have a basic desire to secure our catch and feel strange after a visit to the local mall if we do not have spoils, in the form of shopping bags or boxes to bring home. While fully appreciating that the latest electronic gadgets and household appliances are consumerist traps with ever-accelerating obsolescence, it is living in a kind of prison when we cannot afford them even if we want to. Living hand-to-mouth, with barely enough money to survive from day to day is like drowning on dry land. If our sense of security is based on high income and status symbols, then Saturn's passage here can be most humbling. Cutting corners and plain stinginess on the other hand rarely lead anywhere good, while dubious money-making plans may also be exposed for their lack of real use or substance.

Saturn helps us when we help ourselves, so this can be a time to face facts and make some positive economies. Cutting down on pointless luxuries need not mean a poorer quality of life; often quite the reverse. We can still buy the best, or nearly, but a little extra efficiency and shopping around means we have the satisfaction of *not* paying over the odds. Many things do not cost as much as we feared, and we may successfully query a large bill, for example, or get a fine overturned. Instead of expecting the worst every time a letter from the bank arrives, it may contain good advice on some savings, or even notice of an unexpected windfall. Avoiding essential expenses for as long as possible does not necessarily make the final bill smaller in any case, especially if it is only our temporary anxiety about money that prevents us looking into the issues properly. We need to keep the faith under this transit, that a pie expands during baking and casting our bread on the waters brings it back buttered.

Bill Gates dropped out of Harvard to form Microsoft in February 1977, precisely as Saturn's hit his Second house cusp. Though he eventually scraped enough money together to reimburse his parents for his college fees, the initial move cannot have come without some uncertain financial moments. The easy way for Gates would have been to continue his studies and become a lawyer, but he saw the future and took a risk. As Saturn hit his Eleventh house cusp in January 2000, Gates announced the 'Bill and Melinda Gates Foundation', the largest charitable fund in the world, pouring billions of dollars every year into heath, education and research.

The section of **Sir Richard Branson's** autobiography covering Saturn's transit of his Second house is entitled 'Living on the Edge'. Between 1978 and 1980, Branson's company Virgin lost large amounts of money, and his own story details the radical belt-tightening measures he took at the time: selling cars and houses, leasing out recording equipment and making staff redundancies. Branson split with his long-term business partner at the time because his own instinct was to borrow heavily and for Virgin to trade its way out of trouble. This occurred in the approach to his Saturn return in the Second house in 1980, and by 1981, Virgin's cash balance had been restored 'almost as quickly as it had run out'.

Saturn transiting the Third House

The issues of the Third house do not at first appear as urgent or essential as those of the Second. Once Saturn has been through the Second house the individual is probably more financially established, or at least his furious preoccupation with money has subsided. So there is a greater feeling of solid ground under a man's feet and he can focus instead on a subtler area where the mind, mentality and thinking come under scrutiny. Fittingly, perhaps for the house relating to versatile Gemini, the Third house is extremely diverse and takes in a wide range of mundane affairs.

The nature of the Third is to take in aspects of our own life that we usually take for granted. It highlights day-to-day thoughts and communication, not in the profound, philosophical sense of the Ninth house, but simply the means of conveying and receiving information. In physical terms, there is a strong feeling of Saturn reverberating around in our own skull. The actual process of thinking and arriving at a conclusion comes under scrutiny and in the classic Saturnian sense, we 'watch ourselves watching ourselves'. Trivial things like being unable to summon up a name or phrase, or tripping and stumbling over our words happen frequently and take on exasperating proportions. We may start to talk more slowly and deliberately, thinking much more carefully about what we say. Or our speech itself takes on a more formal or professional quality, taking media training for example to learn how to put ourselves across in pleasing, modulated tones. Strong fences, it is said, make good neighbours. Troublesome neighbours do not seem like much of a problem until we experience them for ourselves. Noise, harassment, and simple lack of consideration all conspire to make home life very difficult; at times unbearable, the more so because it is impossible to escape. Without becoming too introspective, it is worth considering if a particular local nuisance under this transit is trying to tell us anything. Neighbours from Hell may be a reverberation from our own mind into the environment, and the reflection of our own inner desire to move or change. Whatever the underlying cause, many people end up fleeing their neighbours or neighbourhood under the influence of Saturn in the Third.

Saturn always wishes to make a statement of his presence, so this may be a time when writing takes a more prominent role. From something as mundane as starting a diary or journal, to more professional projects like magazine articles or writing a book, we become more focused and disciplined. The first advice usually given on specialist writing courses is, of course: *actually write*. A kind of irony has grown up around the claim of 'planning a book', but Saturn transiting the Third house is the time when we put the concrete physical effort in. The prospective author has a vivid imagination and an abundance of inspiration, but still has to invest solitary hours, with all the attendant mental planning and execution.

Professional writing appears a highly idealistic vocation, but soon brings an acquaintance with the dread deadlines. Very often, commercial writing is done somewhat by rote and we feel very keenly mental effort of meeting the word count for another formulaic article. The crank turns. There is a suffocating feeling of having to conform to a narrow remit and the very Saturnian pressures of time and expectation take us back to being a child suffering with homework. Writing can also be quite therapeutic, of course: thinking through issues and having something to refer back to afterwards, is a way of getting some perspective, especially if something important is going on. Saturn has a way of allowing us to bring mental processes out into the world: to make the inner life visible and tangible.

Education is another Third House affair, except not in the Ninth house sense of University or higher education, but more mundane schooling and tutoring. This transit may be a time when we want to share our knowledge with others, but the nature of the Third is that we may have to teach at a lower level: children, or people with elementary skills. We go in with visions of leading a class of mature and committed students, earnestly discussing high concepts and classic literature, but end up teaching basic skills to a remedial class. For some, teaching special needs are a vocation, of course, and this may be the point where we first hear our calling. Schoolchildren often experience a difficult time during this transit. A Gradgrindian emphasis on facts, facts can be oppressive in the extreme and the whole school environment can seem alien and threatening. Bright children do not necessarily fit in with the educational standards and there may be a sense of underachievement or unfulfilled promise. Parents with school-age children should pay close attention to their children's fears and problems if any of them are experiencing this transit.

Of course, we may be the ones taking a basic course of education, especially in technological times where we must keep up with the latest advances. Computers are a Third house issue, something that has injected a whole new meaning into this area. Not only do we have to organise our ideas, accounts, or fictional works, but we also have to master the keys that bring them all to our fingertips. For most people, computers are simply a tool, but Saturn transiting here is a time when they become more than a means to an end. The intrinsic abilities and limitations of information technology can determine our success or failure at this time, which may bring a certain amount of frustration as the screen machines take on an oppressive and tyrannical form. Yet it is no good going the other way and having a desktop that resembles an aeroplane cockpit, if all we wish to do is create a few simple documents.

Siblings are the other main matter of the Third house, and all manner of questions arise under this transit. Some people experience their brothers or sisters as a burden or worry, while others may be doing very well working together in a family business context. There is a hierarchy in most sibling relationships, usually according to age, and the classic rivalry may arise, especially if a younger family member becomes more successful and starts making their presence felt. Alternatively, the dutiful elder brother or sister takes on a quasi-parental role and lays the law down in a Saturnian fashion, perhaps becoming quite bullying or overbearing. Such dynamics survive well into adult life and it may take this transit for a younger individual to stand up and assert himself, or else to grow up and take more responsibility.

Charles Dickens made the transition from journalist and court reporter to a literary career as Saturn crossed his Third house cusp. His first novel, *The Pickwick Papers* was published in 1837, followed shortly by *Oliver Twist* and *Nicholas Nickleby*, all under the same Third house transit. Dickens's prodigious output reflected his natal Saturn in Capricorn, while Saturn's Fourth house placement also manifested in his difficult childhood and later domestic life. Children escaping from their harsh upbringing of course formed one of the defining themes of all Dickens's work. Journalist **Martin Bashir's** infamous 2003 television interview with Michael Jackson was broadcast while Saturn transited Bashir's Third house. This television documentary feature, where Jackson admitted having teenaged boys in his bed, formed the basis of his subsequent conviction (and acquittal) for child molestation. Bashir himself was subjected to criticism for his perceived entrapment of Jackson, and whatever the truth of the programme, a general breach of trust.

Saturn transiting the Fourth House
'Darkness on the Edge of Town' – Bruce Springsteen

Saturn entering the fourth house domain represents a tour of the bottommost part of the horoscope, where the integral elements of roots and security come to the fore. This is an especially important transit inasmuch as it provides an anchor for life and we can establish a secure foundation to the pyramid of our future success. The Saturnian quirk of fate comes in the form of an organic change of environment, which appears to come out of the ether and it becomes time to simply move on. Perhaps a feeling has been brewing for some time that we need a change of scene, for several different reasons. Saturn's transit of the Third house may represent problems with the immediate environment, so a change of location seems to be a natural progression. Noisy or disagreeable neighbours represent an echo from our surroundings, which reflect a general inner dissatisfaction, and a prompt towards domestic change.

The home base is a crucial part of life, far more than simply providing a roof over our head. As a soul lives in a body, a body lives in a house. The home is our exoskeleton, and the right location, orientation and general domestic atmosphere make a crucial difference to all-round success and happiness. Moving house ranks only after bereavement and divorce as the most stressful of all experiences, for there is a sense of being physically, emotionally and psychically uprooted. There may be a difficult domestic atmosphere for whatever reason: a strained relationship, or memories from the past that seem to require a physical move in order for the ghost to be laid. Either through a desire for a better or more affordable home, to be near relatives, to leave a relationship, or for any one of a range of factors, it becomes necessary to relocate.

The abstract ideal of this transit is to find a sense of belonging wherever we happen to be, though this may be asking a great deal. Depending on the natal chart, anyone having planets placed in the fourth is much more likely to want a haven or somewhere secure to retreat into. A nomadic life is good for a time, but Saturn entering the Fourth is the point where we wish to settle down.

Conditions seem to demand unexpected moves, perhaps serially relocating from one place to another before there is an opportunity to be grounded. This is disruptive at the time, but looking back, we may be glad of the change of scene and appreciate that it might never have come without the intervention of fate. Once again, the home is our base of operations, and once this is right, success is more likely to follow.

Home ownership comes under the Fourth house banner of course, and dealing with estate agents and building societies are the currency of this transit. Very often the home base is a source of financial investment and we have to separate out our own feelings of comfort and security against the desire to make money. This is perhaps the crux: finding a home base that works and provides a good feeling, as opposed to living where we think we ought to be. Once again, *ought* is a familiar Saturn bogeyman. A well-appointed caravan with a pleasant view may ultimately provide a more satisfying alternative to a high-maintenance trophy home with a crippling mortgage. This is the extreme case, of course, but it may take some time before we discover exactly our own golden medium. It is worth embracing the Saturn challenge and getting it right first time – people move house for all sorts of reasons, but rarely for fun.

The Fourth is also the house of the Father, so this may be a time when family relations come under scrutiny. Problems in our relationship with a father figure, or our father himself having problems is magnified in our minds and this may be a source of worry or difficulty. Young people still living with their parents may find the home becoming a more uncomfortable or unwelcoming place. They wake up to the reality rather than seeing it reflected through a rosy, childlike, domestic ideal. The projections that we had always carried around of the father figure come up against his actual qualities and we have to separate out the two. Going against the expectations of our home background in general and our father in particular can be a significant struggle. Seeing this powerful, archetypal Saturnian figure as simply a fellow soul is one of the classic growing up experiences.

Jeddu Krishnamurti was the 'boy messiah' brought from India to England by Charles Leadbeater and Annie Beasant of the Theosophical Society in 1909. The Theosophists dreamt that they had discovered Maitreya, the new Buddha, and set to work educating the fifteen-year old boy and sending him on exhaustive lecture tours. Saturn transiting Krishnamurti's Fourth house by 1912, must have emphasised the strangeness and alienation of his new surroundings in snobbish Edwardian England. During Saturn's fourth house passage in 1913, he was rejected for study by the Universities of both Oxford and London, reflecting his natal Ninth house Saturn. This same natal placement no doubt lay behind Krishnamurti's own much later renunciation of his intended role as World Teacher.

Dylan Thomas wrote his famous poem on his dying father, 'Do Not Go Gentle Into That Good Night', in 1951, as Saturn transited his natal Fourth house. Its refrain, 'Rage, rage against the dying of the light' is the perfect reflection of Thomas's natal Saturn-Pluto conjunction in the Twelfth house.

Saturn transiting the Fifth House.

The fifth house is such a fundamental part of life and the feeling of being alive, that Saturn transiting here is among the most challenging phases of all. Chronos's myth is depicted against the backdrop of children and the family, which on one level are simply manifestations of re-creation. The individual's attitude toward that which he has created comes very much into focus at this point and perhaps the main moral of the story is learning to love what he has made. While in many ways it is the most self-centred and ego-oriented house, its central matter, children, require sacrifice and self-denial on the part of the parents. Still, the reward for this is pride and love, and also a sense of purpose. Though it is in no way a philosophical area in the Ninth-house respect, creativity in all its various guises elevates life out of a dour, pointless struggle for existence.

Children are the dominant Fifth house matter, and this transit is the time when many people work hardest at bringing them up. The Fifth is the house of drama and self-expression and there is nothing so completely egocentric as a small child. Abandoning a starring role in our own drama to give unconditional love and attention to such adorable self-centred little tyrants is a trial to even the saintliest person's patience and this transit is where medals for parenthood are potentially won. A career may have to be radically altered or abandoned to work around the child's routine and it is a struggle to find enough hours in the day. This may be enormously frustrating and finds parents resenting their children for the intrusion into their time and freedom. This is an uncomfortable notion, though it highlights the fact that parents rarely hate their children intrinsically. It is rather that they hate the limitations on their freedom that children impose and the complicated feelings they arouse. Children can also bring out the absolute best in people and have an almost miraculous ameliorating effect, especially for people with a difficult natal Fifth house. No doubt children can be a worry at this time. Pushy parents have become something of a comedic figure, but a child carrying its parent's hopes, dreams and fears is one of the most emotive of all archetypes. Some people work very hard at getting pregnant during this transit, taking fertility treatment or other measures to help them start a family. Parenthood becomes an absolute imperative and for many, there is almost nothing they would not do in order to have a child. Even for those with no intention of starting a family, there is an awareness of the awesome responsibility of potential parenthood. A fleeting Fifth-house love affair, or one-night-stand, perhaps, proves to have far greater consequences than was imagined at the time. Other people may be working very hard to *avoid* getting pregnant, and there may be a vague feeling in the back of their minds that it would be very easy to do, yet most unwise. Saturn in the Fifth house, either by natally or by transit does not necessarily prevent pregnancy per se, but in Saturn's usual way, delays it or represents a challenge once the baby has been born.

There is a sense in which creativity is a kind of neurosis, at very least an escape from the everyday world. The extreme highs and lows of performance and inactivity, acclaim and obscurity are such that the infamous pressures can be quite hard to bear. So many myths build up around the area of the arts, which of course can assume any number of means of expression. An artistic vocation is a precarious thing, which does not have a royal road to fulfilment. Neither the finest education, nor the most prestigious academies can guarantee a career in the performing arts, and in any case there is often a quite distorted impression of the perceived glamour of life on the other side of the velvet rope. Pressures, expectation, media intrusion, financial insecurity, living out of a suitcase: none of this appears in the brochure when a would-be performer runs off to join the circus. Saturn transiting the fifth house can be the time when the distinction becomes most apparent and a balance must be struck between conventional work and creativity.

The desire for creativity usually carries with it an ambition for fame, and it is true that one without the other is a somewhat empty experience: both performance and acclaim are equally Fifth house issues. Play and creativity are two central aspects of the Fifth house, areas where Saturn has mixed fortunes. In terms of sport and play, Saturn qualities are seen in a rather dubious light: frequently successful, but equally often boring - Saturn loses here even when he wins. The public prefers the maverick sportsman in possession of a rare and unpredictable gift, to the Saturnian sort who plays it safe – *and still wins*. Still, this transit is where we inject a little professionalism into our play, practising hard and not relying on passing whims and good fortune. The professional is the person who can do it twice.

The same applies to creativity and the arts. This is the time when the artist snaps out of the temperamental, amateurish attitude and starts to put some actual work in. Musicians in particular are notoriously lazy, yet anyone who does not give up at this point may aspire to more than being the latest darling of the Club scene or the music press. Instead, they set their sights on more mature and lasting goals; outstanding live performance, a number one album, or receiving an annual armful of Grammy awards, in full evening attire. Merit in any art form is highly subjective, and the only ultimate measure is longevity. The public loves the latest trends, but quirkiness dates very quickly and the art that tends to survive has the best kind of classic, conservative Saturnian qualities. Even for those without starry-eyed notions of fame, this transit may be the time to take that first faltering dance class or piano lesson. Music teachers, for example often report that students turning up for a lesson after a day at the office are amazed and delighted at mastering even the most rudimentary tunes and techniques. Company men coming out of a stiff suit and tie world look upon the humble guitar teacher with touching faith, as a great shining Guru. Creativity and self-expression is positively therapeutic, on however small a scale and helps open up part of the soul.

Woody Allen began an affair with his adoptive daughter, Soon-Yi Previn during Saturn's transit of his Fifth house. At around this time in early 1991, Saturn had just conjoined his natal Mars and was separating from a square to his natal Venus. This occurred in the context of Allen's natal Saturn in the Seventh house, highlighting the nearly forty-year age difference between himself and Soon-Yi. Something was clearly wrong in his relationship with Mia Farrow, perhaps he was lonely, but in any event, the temptation was too strong to resist. The outcry once the relationship was discovered was intense and highly public, including unproven accusations of child abuse and a subsequent custody battle over Allen and Farrow's other children. Much of this occurred while Saturn transited over Allen's natal Moon, and the approach to his second Saturn return. Allen and Soon-Yi were eventually married in 1997, while Saturn transited through Allen's natal Eighth house.

John Lennon entered into a period of semi-retirement from music as transiting Saturn entered his Fifth house in 1975. The ostensible reason for this was to effectively trade in his creativity to devote time to his young son, another Fifth house concern. Whether his muse had in fact dried up, or else he felt he no longer had anything to prove, he released no new music for the next five years. He claimed that this was a liberating experience which released him from the pressures of fame and his public persona (natal Saturn in the First house). This fallow period took in part of Saturn's transit of his Sixth house, where he was apparently a contented house-husband, baking bread and embracing macrobiotics and other fad diets. By the time of his assassination in 1980, he had taken on a positively gaunt and ascetic appearance.

Saturn transiting the Sixth House
'Life is what happens when you are busy making other plans' John Lennon.

So often overlooked and underrated, the Sixth House is in fact the engine room of the horoscope, governing the integral issues of work, health and routine. The apparently *most* mundane of mundane houses' rulership of technique and adjustment to necessity can be understood more clearly by seeing that attending to the Sixth's affairs helps us get more out of all the other houses. Whatever the specifics when Saturn drops in, developing a 'Sixth sense' enables us to gain mastery over important matters that are otherwise ignored at great cost.

Rather than work and health, the Sixth used to be known as the house of *sicknesse and slavery*, and of all transits, Saturn passing here reminds us why. A job here may represent a bridge to get us to the ambitions we really want to pursue - probably something represented by the Mid-heaven or planets in the Tenth House. The Sixth house relates to humble fill-in positions as opposed to true vocations; means to ends, not ends in themselves. We talk grandiosely of working on creative projects, but in the interim we have to pay the rent. Aspiring actors or musicians, for instance, with extravagant natal First or Tenth houses, may be found driving minicabs or waiting on tables during this transit, with a faraway look in their eyes.

The Sixth house rules in-between days. This is one of its most frustrating elements, especially if there is great career ambition – yes, we have work to do, but it often involves long hours, low pay and little intrinsic satisfaction while we fill in time. Saturn's transit here develops a pragmatic approach and the need to accept work where it comes and on the level that it is presented. All very fine and sensible, but low status, wage slavery and tedium are the obstacles we face in order to work through it. Alternatively, this may be a test for the individual who is not quite ambitious enough. If our working pattern has been for temporary positions, or moving serially from one day job to another, then this transit may bring frustration until we look for something more meaningful. This does not imply searching for superstar status with a fat salary necessarily, but rather work that is a little closer to the heart. The Sixth is about providing essential service and if we keep this in mind, we learn important lessons about developing excellence without needing our name up in lights.

Job satisfaction is an absolutely central element of physical wellbeing. People who enjoy their work are happier, healthier and live longer: fact. Demanding, stressful work has a definite psychosomatic effect on the individual's health, especially if there is no intrinsic appeal to their task. At other times, working long hours and generally running ourselves down result in ailments and illnesses that could otherwise be avoided. This can be among the most grinding and frustrating of all Saturn transits, with the feeling of futility and crushed-ness and simply existing from day to day. It requires a degree of patience, as always, and a wider perspective that keeps in mind the reason why we are doing a particular job. Losing this perception makes any service we provide mere slavery and, if possible, it may be better for anyone in this situation to cut their losses and leave.

Health itself is of course the other main Sixth house concern and this is the time we start working on it. The body loves routine, which is a Sixth house issue in itself. We diet, detoxify, and generally embrace new regimes designed to drum us into shape. This transit may represent a rehabilitation programme, a course of physiotherapy perhaps or a programme of drugs, prescribed or otherwise, on the slow, Saturnian road to recovery. This may apply especially to broken bones, of course. Repeated ailments may be trying to tell us something and we learn a great deal about ourselves through the obstacle of ill-health. There is a profound karmic dimension here, and for many people a serious or prolonged illness is a crucial turning point in their life, through which they become a different person. This is another reason why Saturnian dues in this domain can be so important.

Tenants and paying guests also come under the Sixth's banner and perhaps only those who have had lodgers truly appreciate the issues that can be thrown up (this latter expression is used advisedly). There are various reasons for letting out a room or house, though any money we make through it is invariably well-earned. Being a landlord is the single greatest cause of human enmity and people rarely enter into these arrangements except by necessity, which is of course the Sixth house style. Look to Saturn's transit here to bring out the interesting issues.

According to his autobiography, **Anthony Kiedis** has Libra rising, with natal Saturn in the Fourth house. The lead singer of the Red Hot Chili Peppers had a complicated relationship with his father, an eminent LA drug-dealer, for whom Anthony became an adolescent bagman, sampling the merchandise all the while. This was the beginning of his decades-long involvement with hard drugs, illustrated in his natal chart by an escapist Sun-Neptune conjunction, in a T-Square with Mars and Saturn. As Saturn transited his Sixth house through 1995-7, Kiedis alternated chronic heroin binges with intense physical exercise and periods in full-time drug rehabilitation. This was a period of marking time in the Chili Pepper's career, after their initial breakthrough but before their eventual world-wide commercial success. It was also at this point at the end of 1996 that Keidis became a vegetarian, after meeting the Dalai Lama in India.

All-time great athlete **Carl Lewis** became a *vegan* precisely on his Saturn return to the Sixth House in July 1990. His new diet was a complete departure, especially for a power-sports competitor, where all conventional wisdom had previously pointed towards consuming large amounts of animal-based protein. Lewis claims not to have noticed any ill-effects, and demonstrated it by working extra hard, and setting new world records for the sprint in 1991, his best-ever competitive year.

Saturn Transiting the Seventh House

'Oh me, what eyes hath love put in my head. That hath no correspondence with true sight'. Shakespeare, Sonnet.

Relationships are one area where many people see the workings of fate most obviously and Saturn transiting the Seventh appears fated indeed. Exalted in Libra, Saturn has an indirect affinity with the Seventh house, suggesting a kind of propriety in the obligation and responsibility entailed in a long-term relationship. The Seventh is the house of contractual marriage, qualitatively different from the fun and frivolity of the fifth house love affair – the Seventh is about life long commitment, sharing, security and status, issues that in their very nature speak in a Saturnian tone.

Saturn transiting the Seventh house for the *first time* in an adult life signifies a relationship and it is fairly safe to count on it. Even if a man is shipwrecked on the remotest rock in the ocean, or has retreated to a solitary Himalayan cave, somebody would have a way of arriving and reflecting him back to himself. A karmic catalyst enters in with the apparent purpose of making him aware of his deepest relationship needs. The feeling of fate to these encounters is very marked, and may be accompanied by an overpowering sense of *deja-vu*. Even the kind of person who prefers to be on his own, may find it very hard to stay out of involvement at this time, while anyone in a relationship when

Saturn enters the Seventh, finds it just got more serious. Both types, even those who have been single for a while and may be quite content, discover someone and perhaps end up living together, though the liaison at first takes on a slight feeling of formality.

Transiting Saturn here is the time above all when we learn that it takes more than love to make a marriage work. Matrimony is a distinct possibility however, and the thought at least is almost certain to arise in some form or other. Given the Saturnian context, marriage takes on a serious and contractual side and there are possibilities of a 'political union' – getting together with someone for hard-headed motivations of money, status or security. It seems as if cohabitation is not enough and we attract a person for whom marriage is an absolute imperative. The relationship has to grow and be taken on to another level, or else it hits a reef. If both parties are prepared to enter fully into such an arrangement, then there is a prospect of success, though this is commonly more to the satisfaction of one person than the other. Whether it is *advisable* to marry now is more open to question and probably depends on the condition of the natal chart. Many people go through terrible agonies *deciding* whether or not to marry, yet the doubt itself implies the answer. The feeling of wanting to bond and make a statement of a relationship is powerful during this transit and the circumstances are often compelling, but the impetus is likely to be much less strong once the transit has passed.

The love triangle is another common manifestation of this transit. This is classic Saturn, where a complicated structure or arrangement has to be created because people want more than one thing. The notion of 'either-or' again outweighs 'both-and'. Either *we* become the mistress or the other man, or someone we are with is keeping their options open. Some people can exist with this and actively enjoy the drama, but it can equally become a quite degrading situation. The *ménage à trois* typically involves both a Saturn partner providing security and a rival offering more in the way of fun. The person in the third corner switches between the two poles, always wanting something their present partner cannot give, but refusing to make a definite choice. Somebody decides they prefer a little more security, or is fed up with a too predictable love life. Either party, husband, wife, lover or mistress may be the one having a Saturn Seventh house transit. The triangle may come about initially through a quirk of fate; perhaps somebody we have known from the past re-emerges to provide an alternative, and ultimately to demand a definite choice. This may occur at the onset of the Seventh house transit, or Saturn arriving here signals the end of the affair.

At a quite profound level, Saturn in the Seventh teaches us what we really want from a relationship, and realise what aspects of our 'other half' are real and what are projections emanating from ourselves. Much has been written in astrological literature about what in Jungian parlance is the animus and anima, and this is the transit almost above any other where our own Inner Partner becomes real and actualised, separate from the image we see in the person we are with[15]. A partner truly becomes our own reflection: our right mirrors their left, and any accusations on our part turn out to be buried deeply somewhere in our own behaviour. The main message here is that in a romantic affair, we basically fall in love with ourselves and hang our pre-programmed expectations on the hook conveniently provided by our partner. Nothing new in this realisation: love poetry and sonnet sequences have celebrated and lamented such infatuations for centuries.

Those who have had this transit, or have Saturn natally in the Seventh, readily recognise the experience of the apparently 'perfect partner' who nevertheless turns out not to be The One. This person ticks all the boxes in the ideal partner inventory: age, looks, interests, Sun-sign, yet strangely fails to move us in any special way. This is a Saturn experience. Saturn is not big on spontaneity and does not allow for considerations of x-factor, spark, chemistry, or other romantic chimeras. With determination, we might carry on a relationship with this objectively eligible person, though with a dawning realisation that something is amiss. Conversely, we may wind up in a long-term relationship with someone possessing *none* of the objective, idealised qualities. An apparently unglamorous partner provides the crucial emotional security, companionship and sense of reliability we want; and we find we simply get along. Wild romances are emotionally draining: they are hard to come by, frequently short-lived, and then take a long time to recover from. Rather than settling for less or selling ourselves short, Saturn brings a mature realisation that marriage is for the long haul and getting our essential needs met is the most important thing.

Open enemies are another kind of Seventh house relationship. We may learn as much about ourselves through a Nemesis as through a saviour. Enmity is of course merely an inverted form of love, and a form of subjective involvement, often for the long term. A divorced couple may be at war with one another for years, especially if there are mutual connections; in-laws and children. The same kind of dynamic to a love marriage still applies, with

Saturnian projection often playing an even more significant role. Some people are motivated by having a bitter rival as a shadow to define themselves against. They need to feel better about themselves, and should this convenient negative image depart the scene, they immediately cast someone else in the role of their adversary. This transit may coincide with a lawsuit, or a time when we need a third party to intercede on our behalf. Either this, or we spend hours on the telephone refereeing someone else's marriage.

US President **Bill Clinton** had Saturn going through his Seventh house when he was impeached over the Monica Lewinski affair in 1998. Like Richard Nixon before him, Clinton's initial transgression was a relatively trivial matter given greater force by his subsequent denials. Clinton's impeachment seemed to have more to do with his open political enemies' desire to pin something on him than any grievous wrongdoing. He was said to have demeaned the office of the President, however, and the backdrop of his natal Saturn in the Tenth meant that his private affairs were exposed in a quite humiliating fashion. That his marriage was not also destroyed was remarkable, though there was political significance even in this. His wife Hilary, who he married in 1975 at the time of his Saturn return, may indeed have been a very forgiving soul, but had good reason to present a united front for her own future ambitions.

Queen Eleanor of Aquitaine was one of the most powerful women in Europe during the Middle Ages, and one of the great female sovereigns. When she married King Henry II of England at the time of her Saturn return to the Seventh House in 1152, she was eleven years older than he, and already divorced with three children. Despite her great beauty, Eleanor's union with Henry was essentially a dynastic affair. Henry was a quite open philanderer, which incensed Eleanor to the extent that she encouraged their children, the future King Richard the Lionheart, and King John, to rebel against their father (shades of Chronos once again). For this, she was imprisoned for sixteen years. She survived Henry, however, to become the Regent of England in her own right while Richard was away at the Crusades. She is the perfect illustration of the political and dynastic struggles inherent in this placement of Saturn

This is further borne out by the example of **Elizabeth I** and **Mary Queen of Scots**, both of whom had natal Saturn in the Seventh. The issue of marriage, far from a mere romantic arrangement, again has the most far-reaching political implications. Elizabeth clearly felt she was married to her country and her royal status (Capricorn rising). Certainly, it is hard to imagine anyone having to contend with more enemies, both open and covert, than she throughout her whole life.

A more mundane example is **Linda McCartney,** who met future husband Paul as transiting Saturn moved into her Seventh house. Already divorced, with one child, she and Paul married in the approach to her Saturn return. This seems to be a perfect example of someone with a stressful natal Saturn in the Seventh – widely opposed to both Venus and the Moon – defying the traditional pessimistic interpretation and getting it right at aged twenty-nine. The McCartney's marriage was, by all accounts, among the strongest and happiest in show business.

Saturn Transiting the Eighth House '*All argument is against it, all belief is for it'* – Samuel Johnson, [on life after death].

The Eighth is the house of sex, death, and taxes – all the sensitive inevitabilities of life that draw up the deepest feelings and tend to be approached rather gingerly. A disturbing transit in many ways, this is a time when we become acutely aware of our personal mortality, finding a powerful sense of wonder at the miracle and the transitory nature of life. The realisation comes across our consciousness in flashes deep and visceral, that human life is an interface between psychic states and in a physical body we walk a path between worlds. Saturn moving through the Eighth house is where we get down into the bass notes.

Saturn can be an intimidating planet and no doubt, the Eighth house is a spooky domain. Both relate to issues that are considered taboo, so when they come together, our imagination naturally tends to supply a scary violin music accompaniment. A keen awareness of the precarious nature of life may result in, at worst, a kind of morbid hypochondria, so it is perhaps as well to get properly checked out and have any irrational health fears put to rest. Many people prefer not to know if there is anything seriously wrong with them, but it is easy to let our imagination run wild. The *memento mori* may also be something more abrupt. A 'car crash experience' is a pivotal point where we re-evaluate life in the light of a brush with mortality. Perhaps we have over-emphasised the material, at the expense of relationships or self-development and a crucial close call reminds us of what is truly important.

Dealing with the business of bereavement and taking responsibility for wills, funerals and undertakers are a major Saturn experience, going up close and personal to physical death itself. Time spent with someone who is coming to the end of their life, perhaps in a hospital or hospice, is a profound experience, both disturbing and beautiful. It is regrettable that it takes such compelling situations to make people face these exchanges, but better by far to have some preparation than to have a loved one snatched away unexpectedly. We have an opportunity to square away issues and perhaps take time to broach important matters left unsaid. However anguished the scene, those slipping away are allowed to depart in peace and those left behind have an experience that strengthens their soul. Spiritual progress during this transit can be quite spectacular, whatever the motivation. The Eighth in many ways represents the most concentrated form of Saturn fear, but conquering this fear is in effect to conquer death itself.

This transit may be the point where psychic experiences come home for the first time, but in any event, the general sense of an unseen presence may be very strong. Haunted houses and locations have a characteristic heavy atmosphere that is quite easily detected once it has first been experienced. It is as if the air itself has a kind of solid, tangible quality that can be projected upon like a movie screen. Clairvoyance comes under the affairs of this house and sensitive souls may pick up on ghosts, spirits and all manner of mysterious phenomena. It may be comforting to contact somebody who has passed over, perhaps via a medium, though Yogic traditions for example, maintain that we are in fact better off in a body, precisely because we can progress and learn our necessary, evolutionary Saturnian lessons here on earth, unlike the dearly departed who have to wait their turn to come back.

We have become acutely aware of the link between sex and death, especially in this AIDS-afflicted era and start to think again how to approach sex and intimacy. Sex becomes more profound and perhaps scary, as we appreciate the idea of the 'petite mort'. We have to reconcile that conquests and no-strings sex are alluring fantasies, but rarely if ever work equally to two peoples' satisfaction. In the Saturnian world, there are emotional dues in any intimate physical encounter. Instead, the true Saturn style may be to become a connoisseur, exploring and sharing with partners on a deeper level and opening up to love and transcendence through sex, rather than tawdry self-gratification. Sex becomes deep and magical and some Yogic or Tantric practices in the context of a committed relationship are excellent means of applying Saturnian discipline. Celibacy does not in every case mean mere abstinence, but the sublimation of the life force in a spiritual and evolutionary direction.

The Eighth is a progression from, or a consequence of, the Seventh and this transit often represents the financial settlement resulting from divorce. The legal aspect may have been dealt with in the Seventh house transit, but as Saturn enters the Eighth, we are more likely saddled with the cost, both financial and emotional. This varies between a landmark settlement in multiple millions or two people going their separate ways and dividing up the book and DVD collection. In any event, there may be assets and resources that we no longer have access to. This could be from a partner, or something as mundane as not being able to use our work facilities after hours.

Whichever way, Saturn here has a lot to say about our relationship with banks, money men and accountants. This is definitely time to be scrupulous about financial affairs, and to avoid contested wills, loan companies and tax evasion. Many people with important planets in the Eighth House have their own business or are self-employed and Saturn here may be the time when anyone makes the leap into working for themselves. This is a good way of expressing the symbolism of both Saturn, in the sense of self-reliance, and also the Eighth in purely business terms.

George Harrison had this natal placement of Saturn, and shortly before his second Saturn return survived a potentially lethal knife attack at his home. Already weak from his treatment for throat cancer, he was perhaps doubly lucky to survive at this point in 2000, though the cancer returned to claim his life two years later. Harrison had embraced different forms Hinduism throughout his adult life, and by all accounts, planned his final bodily exit with meticulous care and great dignity. Knowing that his illness was mortal, he consulted various spiritual authorities to determine the absolute correct steps and protocols for departing this life. Before his passing, he left precise instructions for his body to be flown in secret to India, and after cremation, his ashes to be scattered on the River Ganges.

In the mid-nineties, as Saturn transited his Eighth house, **Sting** became (in)famous for his Tantric sex exploits. This was in the context of his long-term marriage to actress Trudy Styler. It was also at this time that Sting discovered that his accountant, had 'diverted' six million pounds of his money into undisclosed business ventures and secret accounts. This siphoning off of his vast fortune occurred over a number of years, but the discrepancy originally came to light in 1992, as Saturn was about to enter his Eighth house of tax and accountants. The irony was that Sting had worked for the UK Inland Revenue early in his career, before finding his natal Third House Saturn vocation in teaching, and then, of course in music.

Lee Harvey Oswald assassinated John F. Kennedy while Saturn retrograded through his Eighth house. This was in the political context of his natal Saturn in the Tenth, in mutual reception with a crusading Mars in Aquarius in his natal Eighth house. Oswald won permanent notoriety as a result of his actions, though he was of course himself assassinated during the same transit.

Saturn Transiting the Ninth House

'Any question which has an answer is no longer philosophical'.

This is the time when we want it all to start making sense. For most of the time, pondering the meaning of existence may be a rather idle luxury, where a man falls back on ephemera learned at Sunday school or *The Discovery Channel*, or some occasional bar-propping philosophical speculation. But not any more. Spiritual understanding becomes crucial and Saturn is not content to let our world-view remain purely personal, we have to be able to explain and defend it to the world. This desire may come up with a bump against the realisation that our beliefs cannot be adequately expressed in any case and that philosophy is an attempt to describe something essentially ineffable. This sounds reasonable enough, but it can be a hard thing to reconcile for anyone seeking solace in large perspectives. Arriving at a coherent personal code entails study and travel, extensive reading and much conjecture in an attempt to understand and articulate exactly how we see the world.

Higher learning is a common backdrop for this transit and for students, there is an exhausting round of books, libraries and lectures of every description. Either there is a philosophy that adequately encapsulates the answers that we seek, or we cherry-pick the best parts of several different paths to form our own syncretic faith. The issue of discovering Enlightenment through an undergraduate course or the local evening class's Introduction to Philosophy can be trying in any event. Instead of finding the Meaning of Life, it is common to encounter red tape, bureaucracy and a narrow academic mindset that is more interested in proper scholarship and an exhaustive bibliography than philosophic nirvana. It is not enough to know a fact; we have to prove we know it, and nothing we say can be taken for granted. Saturn focuses the student's initial enthusiasm for truth and teaches him to play by the prevailing scholarly conventions. Until we have reached a certain Saturnian status or attainment, in the eyes of the academic establishment at least, our naïve opinions count for nothing.

Formal education, however, is clearly a major rite of passage for vast numbers of people and few transits so obviously show Saturn's role of Great Teacher. Being given books and tasks we would not otherwise have read or questions we would not have pondered is a microcosm of the general Saturn experience and we emerge from a period of learning as more aware, fully-rounded people. Intuitive convictions are deepened after this experience and we are able to apply our thinking to the real world, knowing far more than our own shallow investigations would have taught.

Many people have basic faith or belief but struggle to reconcile their spirituality with organised religion. Saturn's conservative nature means a spiritual path chosen at this time is likely to be stricter or more doctrinaire in its nature than a nebulous New Age belief. It is comforting sometimes to have definite articles of faith mapped out, rather than be required to come to our own conclusions. People who have been on the fringes of faith, as it were, lay members or non-practicing believers might decide to become more actively involved in their particular path or place of worship. Guilt or a sense of atonement may be at the root of this, though some people equally embrace a less judgemental faith to escape from their previous sin-ridden preconceptions. The initial stages of a new belief may be marked by the zeal of the convert, but this evangelical stance commonly quietens down as Saturn progresses through the Ninth, and the individual becomes more secure in his own convictions. The spiritual awakening under Saturn's influence is likely to be slow, but no less welcome and liberating.

A particular place, region or country that we have visited often in our imagination may be imbued with the qualities of a mythical dreamscape. Treading this country's hallowed ground and breathing its sacred air becomes a kind of pilgrimage, and from a safe distance seems surely all we need for instant Enlightenment. Saturn, however, brings other issues to the fore. Passports, visas, inoculations, unfamiliar food, the language barrier and lousy weather are the companions of the experienced traveller. Saturn does not stand in the way of anybody single-handedly circling the globe, but spiritual illumination does not reside in any particular area and the timeless message is reinforced that no matter how far we travel, we always take ourselves with us. However, Saturn's transit here may bring an irresistible urge to travel, or an overwhelming imperative that cannot be ignored. We are made a fantastic offer of a holiday or more likely, a job abroad, and Saturn conspires so that we *have* to go, have to deal with all the necessary arrangements and cannot simply duck out of it and stay at home. The Ninth is also astrology's traditional mundane house. There are other candidates; the Eighth house of occult art for one, the Twelfth of mystery and enlightenment, or even the Sixth in the sense of a traditional craft technique. But the Ninth represents a philosophy or belief system, which is quite revealing about the practice of astrology. There is something quite comforting about seeing personal problems in a more elevated, cosmic context and the application of astrology to life's pressing dilemmas provides, at its best, a feeling of uplift akin to a religious experience. Saturn, as we have seen, is astrology's most pivotal planet, and even its predisposition to see life in somewhat narrow and fatalistic terms has a more positive reading. Co-operating with destiny and avoiding hubris by showing a little humility in the face of the cosmic design is a spiritually healthy attitude, so perhaps astrology itself has an intrinsically religious or revelatory element.

Muhammad Ali underwent this transit prior to his Saturn return. At this point in 1967, he was still Cassius Clay, his 'slave name', and it was here that he first became involved with the radical Muslim group, the Nation of Islam. He embraced the faith, changed his name and refused to be drafted to fight in Vietnam, which was about the most compelling Saturn call overseas imaginable[16]. Ali's natal Saturn in the Tenth gave his anti-war stance a wider political significance, but by the same token, it cost him dearly in professional terms. He was only spared prison time on appeal, and still had his boxing licence revoked for the three years that should have been the peak of his career. He lost his first memorable bout with Joe Frazier at the time of his Saturn return in 1971, though he was to regain his title a second and a third time, eventually transcending the sport of boxing to become a truly beloved world figure.

William Lilly, the 17th Century master of horary astrology, began his intense astrological studies shortly after Saturn entered his Ninth house. His primary teacher was a mysterious man named Evans, who was also well versed in magical arts: summoning spirits and creating talismans, and much of this lore he passed down to his young apprentice. Lilly had natal Saturn in the Eighth house and some of his judgements in *Christian Astrology* rely on the invocation of entities for their resolution, though he relates in his autobiography that he later had something of a soul crisis and renounced all occult art.

Bob Dylan's conversion to Christianity in 1979 and the evangelical albums and tours that followed encompassed perfectly Saturn's transit through his Ninth House. A transit such as this inclined him towards a more conservative form of religion, rather than the more mystical or left field spirituality usually associated with the rock world.

Dylan has natal Saturn in the Fifth House, closely conjunct his Moon, and this placement cannot be said to have inhibited his creativity in any respect (he has at least five children). But a curious feature of his live work particularly is the apparent indifference with which he delivers his material. To the frequent confusion of his band-mates, songs are rarely performed the same way twice and are sometimes sung in little more than a croak. Even allowing for his signature stripped-down delivery, it sometimes appears that he has little regard for his own back catalogue and he has been quoted as saying it does not even occur to him that he actually wrote some of his songs.

Saturn transiting the Tenth House

'Somehow or other I'll be famous, and if I'm not famous, I'll be notorious'. - Oscar Wilde

After Saturn's transit of the Ninth house, we have a wider and more complete sense of how the world works. Our horizons have been expanded by a period of travel or a course of education and we want to start applying this knowledge to a proper vocation. With an internationalist outlook and initials after our name, we take our ambitions into the career domain of the Tenth house and try to become somebody. The Tenth is an earth house, though not concerned with money in the Second house sense or about daily work like the Sixth, but in the wider social sense of a calling or mission. Lessons are strewn in our path, which seem to ask the question: *'So, how much do you want it?'*

The Tenth is Saturn's home base and his passage across the Mid-heaven traditionally represents the most visible, worldly passage in a life. This is where we are paying most attention to career ambition and trying to make a permanent statement of our skills, aptitudes and achievements. If on course at this time and having followed a suitable path with no shortcuts or hidden skeletons along the way, then success should come to find us. This can be a harvest time, when the rewards for years of patient effort have built up in the karmic bank account and a steep career trajectory seems assured. A mere job or position may be transformed into something more meaningful, as we set up a vocational structure than we can rely on for years to come. Not so much an appointment as a whole life purpose.

Yet it is also important not to 'career' out of control, for the Tenth is equally about public image and reputation and our conduct and comportment up to this point determine whether we are bound for either fame, or notoriety. All kinds of dire warnings are attached to the transit of Saturn through the Tenth, with a whole body of case histories recording those who have attempted shortcuts to their place in the Sun. The more extreme examples of major falls from grace seem to apply to those with a natally afflicted Tenth house, but not exclusively. The higher we climb, the longer and more painful the fall.

We all have a life's mission or calling, though it may be very deeply obscured. People are ambitious for all sorts of reasons, and many start to work through their underlying motivations and understand *why* they have such a strong need to achieve. Aspiration is a noble motive, but particularly marked ambition in a man may be overcompensation for low self-esteem, lack of parental attention, or other past rebuffs. Saturn transiting the Tenth is when we realise these driving forces for what they are and start getting a little more perspective. For this reason, it may seem that nothing much 'happens' in terms of outward events during this transit. Instead of blind office-seeking, we simply take on a new attitude: in this case, realising that status and position do not matter as much as we thought. Who we *are* matters more than what we *do*. Far from giving an easy ride, of course, sea-change insights like these come at a cost: frequently there is doubt, deliberation and setbacks before the psychic breakthrough is reached.

Comparisons between Oscar Wilde and **Jeffrey Archer** on a literary level are tenuous, but their shared path from society's darling to public outcast are linked in their mutual Tenth house Saturn. At his second Saturn return to the Tenth house in 1999, Lord Archer declared his candidacy for the post of the inaugural London Mayor. A ripple of alarm spread among those who had known him for years, and in a classic Tenth house karmic ricochet, his enemies were galvanised into action. As Saturn moved into his Eleventh House, a former friend, who had supplied Archer with an alibi in a 1987 legal case, admitted that this cover story had been a lie. Archer was subsequently convicted of perjury, and during the time Saturn transited his Twelfth House, he served two years in prison. He could presumably have avoided this fate had he not over-reached himself and chased so relentlessly after high office.

Rupert Murdoch is about as Saturnian a figure as can be imagined, and it was during Saturn's transit of his Tenth house in 1981 that he achieved his long-held ambition to buy *The Times* newspaper of London. It seems fitting for this archetypal establishment notice-board to have a proprietor with Saturn rising in Capricorn, yet it did not take 'The Dirty Digger' long to transform the working practices of Fleet Street utterly. As Saturn approached his natal ascendant, Murdoch uprooted *The Times* from its traditional home and transferred it to News International Headquarters in London's East End. Saturn transiting Murdoch's Twelfth house at this point in 1986 seems to have signified a clearing of the decks, in his typically pragmatic and unsentimental way.

Despite other famous examples: Oscar Wilde, John F. Kennedy, Hitler(!), natal Saturn in the Tenth does not always mean a great fall. It does mean, however, that public figures with this stern influence are more or less forced to behave with propriety. **Queen Elizabeth II** is a notable case in point: throughout the toe-curling soap opera that the House of Windsor has become during her reign, she remains dutiful and dignified, never doing anything to compromise her position or that of the Monarchy. While this restraint has earned her widespread respect, Her Majesty has rarely enjoyed overwhelming affection from the public and there is widespread suspicion that her buttoned-up manner has contributed to the dysfunctional state of the Royal Family. Another sad feature of this quintessentially Saturnian character is that she may only be truly appreciated after she is gone.

Saturn transiting the Eleventh House.
'I have a dream today'

There comes a time in a man's life when he has achieved a certain amount in his career – perhaps made a name for himself, or arrived in the kind of job that he has always wanted. Saturn's progress across the Mid-heaven has provided a certain status or self-knowledge and having thus peaked, the individual feels secure and accomplished enough not to need reach for further triumphs. Alternatively, tired of the corporate world, he may decide that being yuppie salary-person is not the way to go and looks for something more inwardly rewarding. Whichever way, he searches for broader and more idealistic aims with a not so narrowly ego-oriented focus, and the Eleventh house of hopes and wishes is the next port of call.

The Eleventh is traditionally a 'good' house, the domain of group endeavours, and given its rulership of Aquarius, Saturn also feels quite at home here. Unless the natal house is in poor shape, this is not *generally* one of the more trying Saturn transits. At the same time, the starry-eyed nature of the Eleventh house vision contrasts very vividly with pragmatic, bottom-line Saturn reality, and as ever, there is a challenge to reconcile the two. People who have operated quite successfully in an idealistic work setting may find corporate or other opportunistic influences intruding into their private Utopia. The political crusade, peace movement and free festival all need money to exist, and hierarchies naturally form between even the most liberal and progressive-minded people. Politics is the art of the possible, but the accusation of sell-out is always present if the real-world compromise is taken too far.

Work-wise, good causes, fundraising and voluntary work often provide the backdrop of this transit, or membership of professional bodies with more or less humanitarian aims. This is entered into with the best of intentions, though what ensues in the altruistic world of Charity often amounts to a crash-course in political intrigue, backbiting, and power struggles. The root cause of this is often the very thing that is supposed to elevate charitable causes to a higher moral plain: the absence of professional status. Most charities are supported by the excellent efforts of voluntary workers and people giving their time and energy for no pay. However, people invariably want some reward for their efforts, and in the upper echelons especially, this usually comes in the form of ego gratification through increased influence or status. In charities, people frequently act on their own initiative according to the amount of free time they have available and expect to wield more power as a result. Grubby salaried employment, on the other hand, has the useful Saturnian effect of clearly demarking professional boundaries, ensuring that people do not overreach themselves.

Peer pressure often becomes an issue, especially for younger people. Having to conform is a Saturnian dilemma, especially if we are thrown together with a group who already have their own private codes and practices. The Eleventh house is very much about our wider context and the sense of standing out in a crowd can be quite uncomfortable. There may be a clique or charmed circle to which we aspire to belong, and yet have to sacrifice some of our own individuality along the way. Likewise, repeatedly bailing out somebody who is in constant difficulty is a good way of discovering who are our real friends. Rising up the ranks in a particular party or cabal requires that we bring people along with us and keep our supporters happy. The political aspect of the Eleventh house once again means we must take responsibility for others and find ways of satisfying everyone with an interest or opinion.

Though **Bob Geldof** has no natal planets in his Eleventh house, the defining events of his life occurred as transiting Saturn crossed his Eleventh cusp. The Live Aid concerts in July 1985 brought a massive range of peers and performers together in a common cause requiring work, discipline, along with Geldof's patented direct diplomacy. Saturn echoed his exalted natal Ninth house placement in the global nature of Live Aid, and also in Geldof's subsequent nickname 'Saint Bob'. Geldof's later agonies in his divorce from

Paula Yates occurred during Saturn's transit of his Seventh house and once again revolved around 'the other man', Michael Hutchence, being an Australian who was then living on the other side of the world.

Dr Martin Luther King delivered his electrifying 'I have a dream' speech in New York on 28th August 1963, as Saturn approached his Eleventh house cusp. In December 1964, with Saturn transiting the Eleventh, Dr King became the youngest ever recipient of the Nobel Peace Prize.

Saturn transiting the Twelfth House – 'Welcome to the Twilight Zone'

The Twelfth's nefarious reputation as the 'house of self-undoing' has two possible interpretations: undoing as in self-sabotage, or undoing in the sense of *untying* a knot in the pursuit of self-liberation. It describes either the mystic or the convict in his cell. Like the Eighth, the Twelfth house has some fairly obscure associations: past karma, sacrifice, self-undoing, dreams, hidden enemies, intuition, isolation; a house that encompasses the whole hidden, unconscious realm and the invisible ether that binds us all. Saturn's passage through here illuminates and solidifies our understanding of this indistinct matter and not the least of its effects is to make us appreciate how much psychic debris we carry around from day to day.

Traditionally the darkest and most malefic of the houses, the Twelfth's infamy comes in part because of its capacity to disrupt personal contentment. This may be unfair, for depending on its condition, the Twelfth is either a rubbish dump or a treasure house, or some point in between, but transiting Saturn is *at first* likely to emphasise its stressful side. Saturn brings the realisation, sometimes quite abruptly, that there is more going on in the unconscious than we are aware and that it is time to do something about managing it. Some people are better adjusted to separation from the general run of life than others, but the sense of isolation and inner emptiness that comes from Saturn in the Twelfth should not be underestimated. Everyday supports: social circle, peer group, employment esteem may be stripped away and we are left with our own resources. People who previously had no time for notions of counselling or self-analysis may find experiences prompting them to at least take a more reflective approach, and also to reassess their attitude to therapy, stress management or anti-depressants.

Many of the unconscious quirks, buried memories and latent fears we carry are remnants left over from previous lives. In a sense of course, the whole chart is simply an aggregate of past incarnations – it's *all* karmic - but the Twelfth seems to apply to specific non-material matter brought over, that in a sense can only be explained by reference to a karmic past. Fleeting, fugitive fears that have hidden in the dark of the Twelfth House for years, or perhaps lifetimes, are brought to our conscious awareness and take on the proportions of monsters dragged up from the ocean bed. Exposing these emotions to the daylight does not come without a struggle and putting a stake through their hearts takes time. These are worries, not of something in the outside world, but of the infinite, inchoate ocean of inner consciousness. In this connection, small events may act as 'triggers' for a period of prolonged soul-searching. An apparently insignificant occurrence, a small setback or upheaval, seeing someone from the past, or simply a change of circumstance appears magnified in our own consciousness and we take some time out to think about the whole matter. This is the signal for a change in attitude and approach to our lives, where our customary way of coping and behaving is fundamentally challenged.

This is often a time when we have to overcome a sense of loneliness, and the task for many people here is to become comfortable with their own company. This is not necessarily achieved by filling the hours out with a manic round of activity, but a more general sense of finding a sense of psychic grounding and forming a relationship with the invisible world. Single people: divorcees or empty-nest parents all realise that we are essentially on our own in the world, yet far from seeing this as an awful void, it eventually becomes quite liberating. Many people who have put up with unsatisfactory relationships for a long time report that even though the adjustment to living alone was difficult, they now appreciate their freedom and could not easily go back to cohabitation.

In any case, the Twelfth House is where the lessons of Saturn are internalised. Swallowing Saturn whole may lead to a kind of morose introspection, even if on a more positive level, seclusion and a general departure from conventional company and social settings bring an essential psychic purge. Solitude is simply the outward behaviour which signifies something is happening on the inner, soul level, and while this may be entered into on a personal whim or inclination, it is equally often a withdrawal for a compelling reason. This is obviously a sharp contrast to the previous transit of the socially oriented Eleventh house, where relationships with people and the wider world are paramount. However, it is precisely for this reason that Saturn moving through the Twelfth can be so difficult.

As well as prompting otherwise outward-looking types of the value of a more reflective approach, Saturn lays down a challenge to those who do look inside. Even those actively engaged in a programme of self-development may find themselves looking to their laurels when Saturn enters this Twilight Zone. Anyone who has been involved in counselling, therapy, or meditation for several years may experience a jolt during Saturn in the Twelfth, where they have to change their approach or try harder. It is not only the unconscious that is stirred, but the means of dealing with it. Major humps in the road, hang-ups and deeply buried fears that may have origins in past lives are addressed and find their eventual resolution. Ironically, Saturn is said to sit well in the Twelfth (traditionally finding his 'joy'), so while this passage may be likened to an extended dark night of the soul, the trials and inner challenges faced along the way are ultimately beneficial and liberating. Erin Sullivan's phrase 'maturing in private' is perfectly apt for this transit, at the most exalted level like the metamorphosis of a chrysalis into a butterfly[17].

One of the most difficult showings of Saturn transiting the Twelfth house is after the break-up of a relationship. At the best of times, there is nothing quite like passionate affair to get to the core of us and even a short-lived romantic episode can throw up feelings of an intensity quite disproportionate to the length of the encounter. For most people, the end of a relationship is the most common trigger for an emotional crisis, and statistically, more people visit doctors for depression after marital shipwreck than for any other reason. In a period when emotions are still raw and there are perhaps conflicting feelings of guilt, failure, rejection, or loneliness, Saturn sits on the psyche, leading to a pensive, brooding self-absorption. It is as if the break-up has been deliberately timed to act as a catalyst, forcing us back on our own resources. The end of a relationship often means we break away from mutual friends, people we knew while in a couple and perhaps our entire social circle, which further aggravates a sense of isolation.

Hidden enemies also come under the Twelfth's banner, which can often mean ways in which we unconsciously trip ourselves up, but can also signify something more sinister. The Twelfth rules the ether that connects us all and Saturn transiting here may be a time when our inner boundaries need strengthening, especially in view of another Twelfth house matter: Witchcraft. This rather quaint assignation may provide sophisticates with a knowing laugh, but as anyone who has been in a New Age shop recently knows, it is hard to get about without tripping over the latest best-selling book of spells. Spells are purposely focused intent for generally selfish ends, and while many people are quite comfortable with the idea of remote healing and sending positive thoughts, the opposite is equally possible. The popularity of many books of spells presumably means such stuff is not only read, but practiced by fairly large numbers of people, not all of whom are especially wise. Astrology and astrologers attract loose cannons like electron magnets, and psychic self-defence during this transit of Saturn is a skill worth topping up and taking seriously.

The Twelfth is like a gateway between states - if the zodiac is seen not as a circle, but a *spiral,* the Twelfth is the point at which we move up on to the next level, like a lift between the floors of a building. Life seems slightly unreal, especially in retrospect and there is a feeling of being tightly enclosed, in a semi-dream state, hard to escape from, with the course ahead obscure and hard to navigate. Ultimately however, this is a liberating experience, from which we emerge lighter, freer and clearer, and many people make more inner, spiritual progress at this point than at any other time in their lives. Personal concerns that seemed so weighty and accusing at the onset of the Twelfth house passage are eventually seen in a more reasonable light, to the point of vanishing. Again, this is very like waking from a dream or the distorted perspectives we have at three o'clock in the morning: the nightly images and phantasms that bent our problems out of shape fade, and we find ourselves wide awake and rubbing our eyes in the dawning light.

Saturn going through the Twelfth house was a time when **Frank Sinatra's** life seemed to be disintegrating both personally and professionally. He married Ava Gardner in November 1951, as Saturn transited his Twelfth house cusp. The couple were the loves of each other's life, but their jealous and tempestuous two years together drove Sinatra to the point of breakdown and despair. Apart from the agonies of his marriage, he lost his voice and his record sales declined, and Columbia Records dropped him as a solo artist in 1952. He seemed almost finished, but as Saturn emerged into the light of his ascendant, 1953 proved a watershed year. He split with Ava (though they remained technically married until 1957), infamously earned his Oscar-winning movie role in *From Here To Eternity* and signed a career-defining deal with Capitol Records. Given a crystal ball (or an ephemeris), no doubt Sinatra would not have volunteered for the experiences of his two-year Twelfth house exile, yet how much of the maturity and lived-in feel that defined his later, classic Capitol years were informed by this spell in the Twilight Zone?

Victorian astrologer **Alan Leo** (William Allan) had, famously, a natal stellium in Leo, including Saturn rising, closely conjunct his ascendant. He was in the forefront of the Theosophical movement in the early 20th Century and his prosecution for fortune telling in 1917 proved a landmark case for the subsequent practice of astrology. Leo ran a thriving mail order horoscope service, but became a victim of his own eminence when he was sued under The Vagrancy Act, an English statute of 1824 that effectively outlawed professional astrology[18].

Leo's trial took place at the approach of his second Saturn return, specifically as Saturn entered his natal Twelfth house. In court, he made a good witness and escaped with only a nominal fine, even though under the Act, he could technically have been imprisoned with hard labour. Jupiter in his natal Twelfth house may have spared him this. The upshot was that Leo decided to rewrite his extensive back catalogue of books and personal horoscopes, rephrasing his traditional predictive style in favour of a *trends and tendencies* approach. This had apparently been his long-term intention in any case, but the lawsuit provided a compelling motivation for him to expedite the work. So influential an astrologer was Leo that others followed his Theosophically-inclined direction and the impact of the Mansion House case has reverberated through astrology to the present day.

A possible reading of this affair is that Leo brought the lawsuit upon himself by a kind of unconscious intention. He did not *wish* to be prosecuted, of course, but as an example of Saturn's transit of the Twelfth house, where latent fears and karma are played out in a quite distorted fashion, he became the instrument of a larger destiny. In the event, Alan Leo did not live to see the revision of his work completed, for he died within the year, as Saturn approached his natal Sun. It is hopefully not too melodramatic to see that he acted as a kind of sacrificial channel for the future of astrology. If this is a fatalistic reading, the irony is that astrology became decisively *less* fatalistic as a result and maybe it is this new movement that was striving to get out.

Paul McCartney's natal Ninth House Saturn fulfils nicely the potted aphorism: 'learning experience in foreign countries'. Attempting to enter Japan in 1980 with half a pound of marijuana in his pocket, he was arrested and spent ten days in jail. This happened as Saturn transited his Twelfth house, of course, and personifying both the enlightenment and incarceration aspect of the Twelfth, he spent the time in his prison cell meditating, as he learned in India in the 1960s.

CHAPTER SIX

FATAL ATTRACTION
Karmic Connections

Some argue that a karmic perspective on anything raises as many questions as it answers, but it does provide a simple and effective insight into to underlying motives in many relationships. All close or significant relationships between family, lovers, enemies, down even to the most casual colleagues and acquaintances, have roots going back into previous lifetimes. Some contacts we have are far more obviously karmic, and in these we often see the signature of Saturn. Close conjunctions in particular between one person's Saturn and their partner's personal planets carry a fated quality, and are not for the fainthearted. Whether the aspect be Saturn to the Sun, Moon, Mercury, Venus or Mars; all carry the feeling of a teacher-pupil relationship. Intuitively, we say Saturn is the teaching party, but this is not always the case. Saturn is more overtly the Master or Mistress, but in a convoluted way, they may end up being the one who evolves most through the connection.

As with any fated situation, the first meeting with someone with whom we share a strong Saturn contact is usually memorable. Somebody enters into our world, so familiar that it seems we have always known each other. Perhaps we have. There is an immediate reaction; attraction, repulsion and-or a weird sense of *déjà vu* when we are in their company. Long before we have worked out the astrology, the evidence is there in our own gut feeling. We may have a desire to avoid the person, or an irresistible urge to get to know them. This seems assured. Sometimes the initial reaction against somebody is very strong, and we recoil, making a point of not getting involved. Despite this caution, our original presentiment often proves correct and a drama plays itself out over the course of the relationship. Even if the contact is not an intimate one, the Saturn connection still has some significant role to play in bringing us an important introduction in love or work, or perhaps a hand in denying either.

The uncomfortable truth from a karmic point of view is that, depending on the orbs, the Saturn partner may wish to harm the person whose personal planet they conjoin. They have a desire to, literally, teach their partner a lesson, and to the extent that they act unconsciously, they often cannot help themselves. This is the most disturbing element. Jealousy, competitiveness, fear, or some other more mysterious quality provides the *apparent* trigger, but their purpose seems to be that the other party needs taking down a peg or two. An underlying sense of grievance brought over from the karmic past can be very strong and the Saturn individual has to trust himself not to settle the score. If he is extraordinarily mindful, he may bring lessons and structure to his partner in a controlled and benevolent way. But he has to realise his own potential to harm his partner, *intentionally or not*, and this is clearly a large responsibility to bear. On this basis, he may decide that the situation is not for him. The irony, however, is that even by showing such apparent prescience and refusing to get involved, he may still cause great upset. Somebody with whom we have a strong karmic connection is likely to take this form of 'prudence' or 'discretion' as coldness or outright rejection. The exchange has roots going *way back* and it is not easy to just walk away and remove ourselves from the karmic equation.

Fated encounters like this involve an element of compulsion, where both parties in fact suffer. It takes two. One party *appears* to be the victim, but the person inflicting harm is no less of a puppet. He may in an unconscious, egotistical sense view himself as the avenging karmic angel, but by harming his partner, he harms himself. He gets embroiled in an increasing spiral of troubles, ensuring further suffering, complication and limitation. Once again, it is incumbent upon the Saturn individual in particular to realise his shadowy potential and not to act upon it. In strictly behavioural terms, there is something about a partner that touches a raw spot in the Saturn person; he is made to picture himself always as the dour, sensible, straight-man. This is especially hard to bear for someone who is otherwise a bubbly optimist, and not at all used being cast as Mr Hyde. But carrying this Saturnian projection around gets to anyone over a time and chips away at their self-restraint. They then decide to live up to their role and *really* give their partner something to complain about, letting fly with dark observations and generally leaving them out in the cold. 'Give a dog a bad name': the classic Saturn self-fulfilling prophecy strikes again. Two people unconsciously conspire to become the instruments of fate, the seed of which is present from the start in their relationship.

The Saturn relationship may be with someone overtly Saturnian: older or wiser, but in any event we learn a great deal, even over a short period of time. The lessons stay with us when we have perhaps moved on to a different partner; somebody who is easier to deal with. The feeling if and when the Saturn partnership ends may be mingled relief and regret, but in any event the sensations are acute. The sense of *potential* at the outset may have been great and we are left with a permanent sense of 'if only'. The emotional dues here seem fated in themselves, which may be especially heartbreaking if there is genuine love signified from other contacts in the chart[19]. This testifies further to the sense of it being a continuation of something begun long before. The distress may be so great that two people cannot see each other again, but the relationship in a sense never ends. The enduring Saturn qualities ensure the two people do not forget each other and remain like psychic furniture in each other's lives.

Why do people enter into such gruelling relationships? It is easy to advance theories of early conditioning, parental images, and generally low expectations, and all of these may in fact play a part. But from a karmic point of view, the tighter the aspect, the more obvious and compelling the lesson. In other words, the more difficult and apparently unpalatable the relationship, the harder it may be to avoid. We have important lessons to work out together and the extreme fated quality of close Saturn inter-aspects mean that such relationships come to find *us*.

Synastry aspects must always be considered in the individual's natal context. Difficult Saturn contacts between charts may be more agreeable and manageable for those with a challenging natal Saturn. They do not *wish* to be challenged through their relationships necessarily and many long for someone who provides a little escapism, but this is not always available. It is in the nature of their natal chart to create a successful relationship along more Saturnian lines. The self-reliant Saturn type may find somebody with whom he can share a more distant love affair, which suits both parties very well. This would be intolerable for others, but busy, career-oriented Saturn individuals often want a life as well as a relationship and find the closer and more obviously codependent arrangements rather stultifying. They can manage on their own and do not need somebody to check in with all the time. It is in the nature of such balanced 'arms-length' relationships to be quite mature, which is why a young person with a strong Saturn may have an older partner, and *may* not find a relationship of peers until at least after his first Saturn return.

A wide conjunction between planets, of five degrees or more, may get the very best kind of Saturnian structure, maturity and longevity from such a partnership, but anything closer and the situation becomes increasingly uncomfortable. It cannot be emphasised enough that *the size of orb is a determining factor*[20]. Squares and more especially oppositions do their work as well, providing the same kind of spur they might in an individual's natal chart. Oppositions tend to pull people apart in relationships, rather than throw them together like the conjunction. There may be an attraction, but two planets are just too far apart to really connect all of the time. A structure or arrangement has to be set up to ensure people spend enough time together. Tight trines and sextiles between Saturn and personal planets are priceless for a long-term relationship, where there is a positive loyalty, understanding and support. But easy aspects take care of themselves. Much of the observation in this chapter is based on tight, hard aspects, where one party becomes the embodiment of Saturn agent in a quite tangible and fated way.

In **Saturn-Sun contacts**, the Sun party feels that he has a great deal to live up to. They must not disappoint the Saturn person, and may become somewhat coerced into his way of doing things. The

Saturn individual has much good advice which he also backs up with action, for on some level he may idealise the person whose Sun he conjoins. Saturn is never impractical. He is inspired by the Sun partner and like a business manager, devises an itinerary of tasks for him or her to complete. The Sun person benefits, for there is always the tendency on his part to complacency; to assume that he or she is at the centre of universe and that everyone acknowledges the fact. Yet at the same time, the Sun individual feels Saturn's workaday approach is dull and reductive, and that he does not understand the rare nature of the Sun person's unique gifts. He may also be shocked at the Saturnian's occasional cynicism and base willingness to do whatever it takes to succeed. The Sun is not naive, but feels that simply expressing himself is reward enough, whereas Saturn wants money and status. The Saturn contact can be very good for two people work-wise, but it does not go away when the time comes to relax. There is no down-time, no spontaneity, but constant planning, and this is not why most people enter into a relationship. Between the two of them, there is the potential to leave behind sound structures and lasting achievements, but this becomes a problem if the relationship is all work.

Saturn-Moon contacts. The Moon is possibly the most important planet of all in relationship terms, more so even than Venus. This is for its insight into instinctive, unconscious behaviour, but the trouble with Moon-Saturn relationships is precisely that they are so counter-intuitive. The comfortable emotional rapport that exists between happy couples is notably lacking. The Moon person tries to explain himself and says idly, 'You know what I mean?' to which literal Saturn replies 'No'. A door metaphorically slams. Some lunar souls stick with this arduous dynamic, because they sense that they can evolve, and in so doing become more emotionally mature. There may be status and security for the Moon person, with an awareness of the Saturn 'rock' watching over them, but these come with overbearing demands and expectations. An atmosphere of discipline and constriction may ensue, so overpowering and positively Gothic that the Moon individual grows highly tense and stressed, like a coiled spring. Their spontaneous lunar responses are made to feel childish and silly, and they end up asking Saturn's *permission* to feel. Yet the Moon relies on Saturn all the same and expects him to look after and provide. This, the Saturn person resents in turn and wonders whether their partner wants a lover or a parent.

The Moon enters into such a liaison to gain structure and soundness from Saturn, the sense of building a life up. The overflowing ocean of lunar energy is dammed up and made to flow in a purposeful direction, like an aqueduct or canal. The lunar individual who has been on his or her own for a time encounters a Saturn partner, and things start to happen. Marriage, mortgage, kids, domesticity, all of the things follow which he dreamed of but would possibly never have done without someone actively pressing him. This happens in a more comfortable way under smooth contacts, or at least hard aspects with wide orbs, but is still a feeling that it is time for some discipline. Marriage or some formal structure is likely and the lunar type agrees to this for the same reason people join any institution: for a sense of purpose and belonging. At the same time, the Moon partner has to shape up and may experience the partnership as a kind of boot-camp, with a sense rather like: 'You're in the army now'.

The Saturn individual may idealise the lunar type and in their company feels the hard, cold edges of his personality softening. The Moon radiates an aura of sympathy and sweet soulful vulnerability to Saturn, but at some shadowy level also, the image as someone with the potential to be controlled. This is itself a manifestation of Saturn's insecurity. The Saturn partner does not understand that the Moon's apparently artless manner conceals greater emotional subtlety, in that their every response does not have to be calculated or concealed. In this respect, it is the Moon that shows greater maturity and Saturn who learns to flow a little more. Saturn melts in this company, which may involve the literal shedding of many tears. There is also a role-reversal dynamic with this aspect if the Saturn party is a woman. She may provide the structure and security and looks to the man for empathy, comfort and release.

Saturn-Mercury contacts

Saturn-Mercury is an overt example of the teacher-student relationship, but once again, it is not necessarily Saturn wearing the mortarboard and gown. This is not about self-expression so much, nor emotions, affection or sexual chemistry, but the all-important area of communication. Two people may remain essentially fond of each other, but if there is nothing to talk about once the honeymoon phase is over, then the basic connection becomes harder work. The problem may indeed extend into other areas of the relationship. There is nothing more deadly than being bored in a partner's company.

In close conjunction or hard aspect, Mercury tells Saturn the things he does not wish to hear. It is natural for Mercury to be inquisitive and conversational, yet his main mode of interest is the area where Saturn basically struggles. At the same time, Saturn seems always to wave the damp cloth, to be sceptical and pessimistic, if not outright hostile to Mercury's natural curiosity. Saturn recognises Mercury's cleverness, but may be rather wary or suspicious of it, making a point of putting Mercury down. This comes from the familiar shadowy Saturn projection, and Mercury is made to feel equally, if not more, slow and challenged as the Saturn partner imagines himself to be. Once again, this may chip away at the relationship between two people, even if the physical chemistry is dynamite.

These contacts may describe two people who are not speaking the same language, either literally or metaphorically. Perhaps there is an actual language barrier, or else one partner has specialist knowledge that he is either unwilling or unable to share. Either this, or the other party is simply not interested. Conversations here may also carry the stamp of uneasiness and go down paths that seem rather dark and unnecessarily heavy. A chat about last night's soap opera turns into a deep discourse on the social mores, at which point both parties feel slightly awkward. Saturn is not without dry wit, but because the conversation is not usually at a light or frivolous level, having a laugh together may become strangely embarrassing.

There is also potential on a more positive level to bring about tangible results rather than simply talk about them. The Mercury partner is full of bright ideas, and with a smooth contact to Saturn, finds that his notions are no sooner said than acted upon and implemented. Trines or sextiles between Saturn and Mercury also mean that the teaching process is practical, enlivening and two-way. Even with hard aspects, if two partners are willing to work, and perhaps there are other mitigating aspects between the charts, the relationship becomes creative and pleasantly surprising, with the challenge to reconcile two very different points of view. Highly evolved types may also take such challenges on willingly for the sense that they are learning valuable lessons.

Saturn-Venus contacts

The well-known aphorism that Saturn-Venus in synastry represents lifelong friendship[21] is carefully qualified not to say lifelong *love*. Friendship is emotionally cooler, more restrained, and often, in fact longer-lasting. Many durable partnerships are characterised by sturdy Saturn aspects, even the hard series. These contacts may seem rather safe, unglamorous or even boring to some, but a couple with aspirations to stay together for the long term can usually use all the safe stuff they can get. It is wrong in any case, to characterise Saturn-Venus as being exclusively Victorian. Saturn exalts in Venus's sign, and embodies both enduring love and also the quintessential romantic experience of two people being brought together by fate.

As with Sun-Saturn, these contacts are like a marriage between artist and manager. With the conjunction especially, the Saturn party sees the potential in their partner's creative skills, as represented by Venus, and cannot understand why they do not work harder at doing something with them. They devise a programme for the Venus partner to follow, exactly like a coach or trainer, for inspiration is not enough and it will not simply be alright on the night. Saturn insists the Venus party gets the best artistic materials, learns all their lines and becomes note perfect. If the Venusian has personal or public relations skills, then they must paint their smile on and get out there hustling. They must always wear the right clothes and get their beauty sleep. This is intended by the Saturn person in the best possible way and the Venus person benefits ultimately from an injection of professionalism. But it is all rather grim and corporate. Venus does things for fun, not because of a grand strategy.

Saturn is also opportunistic, and there is always potential for him to essentially *use* a partner. He makes a deliberate calculation, and decides that a small sacrifice is worth making if it pays off in the longer term. For sure, his awkwardness is accentuated, feeling very much the clumsy Saturn literalness and ill-humour around the affable Venusian, but to some extent he basks in reflected glory. The Saturn partner portrays himself as solid and dependable; the honest and hardworking Joe, muttering darkly that the Venus person finds his place in life only through a shameless PR campaign. In this, the Venus party is an innocent victim, for *his* charm is usually unfeigned and instinctive, but cannot escape the fickle and untrustworthy Saturn projection. At the same time, Venus is not above trying consciously to beguile the lonely Saturnian individual, especially if he has status or useful skills. A little fun will do him good, they reason, and besides, he has money and a big house. The potential for a kind of courtesan relationship is always present, where Saturn works hard and Venus supplies the personal touch. There is also sense of either partner taking the other on as a work in progress: The Saturnian makes the Venus partner more focused, while learning to lighten up and become a little more stylish himself.

Wherever Saturn is found, there is a businesslike attitude, so

Saturn-Venus often describes either a work-oriented relationship, or a literal partnership between agent and client. Two people with this connection may work together and perhaps find it inappropriate to be overly involved or affectionate while at the office. In any case, the nature of Saturn-Venus means that boundaries are very clearly defined, and the challenge becomes to find time to relax and let go. In a professional relationship, we may enlist the services of somebody who is very good at their job, even if we do not necessarily like or approve of them. Most people, however, do not conduct their business in this rather chilly fashion, and even the most formal business transactions or job interviews beyond a certain point hinge on matters of personal chemistry. As the *I Ching* says: 'affection is the all-important aspect of relating and all unions based on mutual interests hold only up to a certain point'.

Saturn-Mars contacts.

Difficult Saturn-Mars in synastry is heralded by the noise of an old-fashioned needle sliding off a vinyl record. Fingers scraping down a blackboard. Hard contacts here show an essential dissonance and antipathy between two people; often plain, cold dislike. Other Saturn contacts may be finessed, worked around or ignored, but Mars's active nature makes this difficult. Mars is neither accommodating like the Moon nor diplomatic like Venus and he affirms his own existence by provoking a reaction in people. He always has to make something *happen*. This involves poking a sharp stick into stately Saturn's side, precisely where he is darkest and most insecure. The more Saturn backs off, the more Mars attacks.

Victim and abuser are ugly faces of hard Saturn-Mars contacts, though it is not always straightforward which side is which. This dynamic may describe the essentially mild-mannered man who enters into a relationship with a woman who has a history of violent and abusive partners. The man knows of her past and at first is all sympathy, but early the course of their relationship he is disturbed to find the red mist coming down over *his* eyes. He is so alarmed that he decides he must get away. Or the woman who lives with a serial wife-beater at first focuses on his extrovert qualities, rationalising that he is misunderstood and she will be different. She tries to ignore the drunken bully who comes back from the pub every night, even in the face of the eventual restraining order. She takes it and takes it, until she finally snaps and lashes out with the bread knife. He ends up in the hospital, but who is the real victim?

Sex is a pressure valve for Saturn-Mars energy, even though there may be something quite compulsive about a couple with difficult contacts. If for whatever reason sex is not available as a release, the animus backs up and the relationship descends into a kind of domestic cold war. Sex then becomes the nature of the problem and if the aspects are tight or difficult, it may be deliberately withdrawn or used as a means of control. The Mars character may be more driven, and cannot understand why the Saturn party seems afraid to let go. Mars has pride invested in his potency and takes indifference or rejection badly. He is not interested in seduction so much as conquest and becomes frustrated when the Saturn partner wishes to take things more slowly. With smooth contacts, alternatively, strength and stamina combine to describe a couple of sexual Olympians.

Mars exalts in Saturn's sign, so it is wrong to say at least that these aspects have no potential. This may be a very dynamic and business-oriented partnership, and if the division of labour is well balanced, two people should positively enhance their prospects of success. Both Mars and Saturn are pushy characters: Mars overtly so, where Saturn is more calculating. Saturn is more inclined to play the longer game and may subtly control the Mars partner, issuing orders and relying on Mars's energy to carry them out. Saturn makes the bullets for Mars to fire. Mars in fact may relish this role of doer and enforcer. His impulsive energy cannot be bothered with planning and premeditation, and is all too keen to show Saturn what he can do.

CHAPTER SEVEN

ARE YOU EXPERIENCED?

Astrologers, Fate and Saturn Strategies.

People coming for an astrological consultation, perhaps for the first time, are very often focusing on Saturn's influence, generally experiencing heavy, burdensome tasks which they cannot presently see their way out of. They do not realise it in these terms of course, but a little question and answer session usually finds the client having *no trouble at all* identifying with the issues represented by Saturn's transiting position. This goes straight to the heart of the problem, with an involved, intriguing story of frequently operatic proportions from the client. People rarely come to astrologers to tell them how wonderfully well their life and loves are going, and Saturn more than any other factor is the common denominator in their troubles. Without Saturn in the sky, astrologers' casebooks would all be lighter in every sense.

While it is correct to emphasise Saturn's positive side in consultation, there is no sense in minimising how difficult it can be. There are few people so focused that they can take heavy Saturnian events in their stride, something of which astrologers, however well meaning, should not lose sight. Saturn represents inert, or very slow-moving energy and the most demoralising effects of his transits, especially through a difficult house or by hard aspect to a personal planet, carry a sense of frustration. We feel stuck. The effort to move out of the situation seems impossibly daunting, while staying in the same place is no alternative. Something, or someone, we have relied upon for security is no longer there and we are thrown back on our own resources. We are struggling along with our ambitions, perhaps barely coping, at which point life throws us yet another ball to keep in the air. Having to run in order to stand still is a familiar Saturn scenario.

In the same way as beyond a certain point all dangers are equal, after a time the emotional pain most people encounter does not get any worse, it is just a question of how *prolonged* it becomes. Fear, hate, jealousy, depression; any negative feeling will reach a finite pitch of intensity beyond which it cannot seem physically to go any further. The only question is how long it is allowed to continue. If no relief is found, a perilous sense of despair may result, but even this will pass if there is something positive to focus on for the longer term. This may be little comfort in the actual moment, but it helps the client realise that they owe it to themselves to at least try and move on. Pointing out a time in the future when conditions take on an easier complexion is a first step. The astrologer's main purpose is to provide a sense of meaning in the client's experience, and point out that the Saturnian situation is not there to harass or persecute them, but to evolve them and ultimately make life better.

Given a reasonable period of time - sometimes not all that long, a matter of weeks or even days after the final pass of a Saturn transit - it is a different story. Afterwards it is possible to put a heavy experience into perspective in understandable terms, which is a crucial point. Surprisingly soon after a given Saturn episode – a transit to a personal planet or house cusp – new morning comes and the client finds themselves back in the sunlight again, feeling like a different person living in a different country, stronger and wiser for the experience.

This brings home one of the essential boons of astrology, that events are, after all, transitory. Saturn will eventually *leave* and the sense of relief is quite palpable and immediate. We can point out to clients with confidence and reasonably accurate timing that bad feelings and difficult circumstances will eventually simply go away. To be sure, Saturn leaves either a material or emotional legacy to remind us of a particularly grisly incident, but no matter how deeply enmeshed in a difficult episode, once he moves a few degrees away from a given planet or house cusp, problems noticeably slacken off. The difference is like night and day. A difficult chart with many stressful aspects may attract difficult conditions again sooner rather than later, and liberation also depends on our willingness to work. But the ephemeris tells us that there is always a glimmer of hope at a specific and foreseeable point in the future.

It can be a touchy question, asking someone who is in the middle of a crisis: 'What do you think you are supposed to learn from this?', and we should apply some sensitivity. The last thing anyone who has been divorced, bereaved, or made redundant wishes to hear is some smug astrologer telling them that they are not honouring some crucial and life-enhancing aspect of the experience. Upon seeing such transits impending in a client's chart, it may be legitimate to say that they have some 'valuable learning experience' ahead of them, and after the transit is over the client should have realised it for him or herself. But a glib, cavalier attitude from the astrologer during the critical time itself may result in said stargazer being murdered. So even when accentuating the positive, words need to be chosen very carefully. Through this, we may discover that the client's situation is not objectively that bad and it is only their fears that are holding them back.

Astrological ethics decree that the reading should always resolve in hope. This is not mere happy talk, or worse, a form of client manipulation, but a reflection of astrology's Ninth house origins, where we should be uplifted by a sense of the divine. Someone with a stressful natal Saturn is not destined to be miserable or persecuted forever, nor to project their shadow on to others and become a tyrant or dictator in his own turn. A hard aspect of Saturn to a personal planet, The Sun, say, may describe an early sense of inferiority and the attendant overcompensation that is its mirror image. Overcoming these classic coping strategies may take time and experience, but the point of learning astrology is to *realise* this archetypal behaviour and to get free of it.

Astrologers.

We have seen that Saturn is the defining astrological influence, so perhaps no surprise that astrologers are a social group of rather mature years. Various new-age types pay lip service to the stars, but the fact is that astrology is an involved, technical subject that takes years to learn and many people come to it only after some life experience and a few trips around the block. In actual practice, consultations bring a whole range of troubles that need a broader view to be effectively dealt with, and to the extent that astrology is a Saturnian discipline, there is something inevitably missing if the astrologer lacks wider worldly experience. There are exceptions of course, but there should probably be laws banning consultant astrologers practising until after at least their first Saturn return.

Astrology has taken the place of organised religion in many

people's lives, in the sense of achieving a mystical connection with the outside world and finding a sense of a life purpose. Astrology was *part* of the picture before, when one would see an astrologer, and depending on their judgement, perhaps go to a priest or minister afterwards in the hope of diverting God's Will. In Jyotish, for example, astrology is simply that aspect of the Veda which deals with knowledge of the future. The birth chart is used to find upcoming obstacles to self-realisation, and then other means are used to remove them. In the modern secular world, astrology has taken on a more comprehensive role, and simple 'good' or 'bad' judgements are no longer enough. Having one's chart read has become a one-stop-shop experience with the astrologer assuming the roles of the soothsayer *and* the priest. Prayers, mantras, talismans and magic no longer play much of a role in what we do, and without these essential remedies to soften their judgements, astrologers have to be far more careful what they say.

Of course, not all astrologers consider themselves counsellors with a capital 'C', which is as well, because not every client necessarily needs formal counselling. Assuming that everyone who comes for a chart reading wants to explore their inner angst is all very well; some might, but most clients are practical people looking for pointers on their love life, money prospects and for better days ahead. It is sounder practice to start by assuming the client is at least as self-realised and well adjusted as we are, rather than to presuppose their inevitable emotional problems. Too often, it is not the client, but the astrologer, who wishes to explore deep 'psychological' issues, whether or not it is relevant to the client's immediate needs.

This is not to minimise the need for a sympathetic ear. The

astrologer does not need a patient's couch, but a box of tissues sometimes comes in handy. For every client who comes for lottery tips or idle curiosity, there are probably a dozen who are quite seriously struggling and for whom astrology is their position of last resort. Either they come with genuine expectations of answers to their troubles, or are prepared to suspend disbelief for an hour or so and listen to something offering them a sense of meaning. This is probably what makes astrology a vocation: we can have all the astrological knowledge in the world, but what the person in front of us wants is someone who they feel understands. This, however, is not the typical Saturnian response: a Saturn-type astrologer may have great reserves of compassion, but feels it incumbent upon himself to *do* something. Silent, non-judgemental empathy, allowing others to simply be and feel is a wonderful quality, but the Saturn type can appear unwittingly insensitive by insisting probing and meddling, for however good a reason.

Astrologers and Fate

Traditional astrology is Saturnian by nature, dealing with form as opposed to content, objective facts rather than subjective attitudes, plot against character. Twentieth Century astrology traced a gradual but progressive path away from this Saturnian event-oriented view, with the traditional fortune-teller's outlook today seen as something of an anachronism. This is not strictly a modern trend of course: the blunt fatalistic outlook has been criticised throughout history, even from within the tradition itself, and has done great damage to the image and standing of art. Radical pre-dictive statements have become frowned upon[22]; not just through passing fashion, but for reasons. The dead hand of a deterministic astrologer makes the positive *invocation* events for the client more likely, and such negative self-fulfilling prophecies apply especially in relation to Saturn, as we have seen. The astrologer in his popular image as arch fatalist, giving adamantine predictions of immutable destiny is often a rather fatuous figure, presenting an image more enlightened practitioners have had to live down.

The prevailing predictive approach for natal work is 'trends and tendencies', or as pointed out elsewhere in this book, to see transits as signposts, rather than strict causal influences. The furthest extreme of this modern 'psychological' attitude is a kind of divinatory school, whereby the planets have little or no pre-existent meaning at all except that which we choose to embrace[23]. Here, emphasis is placed on the horoscope as a medium for the intuition of the astrologer, and interpretation as a kind of ritual act. Judgement may come unbidden, as it were, as much through the astrologer's prophetic imagination as the minutia of the symbolism[24]. This is summed up in the aphorism: 'it is not the astrology, it is the astrologer'. Such an outlook is in the tradition of ancient divinatory systems like the *I Ching*, which is not so much concerned with *prediction*, as our conduct at the particular moment. The *I Ching* does not speak of unfortunate events; it says 'do not act in this way'. The responsibility is placed very much in our own hands, creating an ethical dimension to the divination absent in the strictly objective approach. Yes, there is fate, but the individual's skilful conduct determines how destiny manifests. This, it seems, is a far more enlightened and constructive approach to interpretation.

Yet Saturn is a thorn in the side of the more liberal believer in fate and reminds us that we do not always have the leisure or leeway to decide how we prefer destiny to manifest. With any number of undiscovered waves, fields and forces running through us, we are more fated and conditioned than most of us probably believe. Saturn represents fate in its most concentrated form and his experience is to 'give' events as if from without. His episodes often *feel* fated, even for those who are ambivalent about the concept. Predictions in one form or other are also what clients expect when they visit an astrologer and we have a long way to go before disabusing them completely of this idea. Astrology is a body of revealed wisdom which allows us a glimpse into the future and 'forewarned is forearmed' is its mission statement. Avoiding a too-fatalistic outlook is not an excuse for astrological practice to have become coloured in various shades of pastel, and the traditional revival in the latter part of the 20th Century may be said to have restored a little of astrology's former dignity.

For even the divinatory *I Ching* speaks of 'Limitation', and its words apply precisely to the astrological Saturn:

In human life too the individual achieves significance through discrimination and the setting of limits. Therefore what concerns us here is the problem of clearly defining these discriminations, which are, so to speak, the backbone of morality. Unlimited possibilities are not suited to man; if they existed, his life would only dissolve in the boundless. To become strong, a man's life needs the limitations ordained by duty and voluntarily accepted. The individual attains significance as a free spirit only by surrounding himself with these limitations and by determining for himself what his duty is.
Hexagram 60, 'Limitation' (Wilhelm edition).

Far from being an either-or situation between free will and fate, here, 'limitation', represented in our astrology by Saturn is the very thing that makes choice necessary. Human life and freewill are all about deciding the best kind of action, which is the basis of all morality.

The debate about fate versus freewill is in fact one across levels of consciousness. All astrologers, surely, believe in destiny, but the extent to which we are puppets of fate depends on our mind level. This is implied in Saturn's essential rulerships of base materialism and fate: by emphasising the material, we automatically strengthen the hand of fate. The two go together, whereas the opposite pole is spirit and free will. The kind of inert materialism Saturn represents is the strata of life least permeable to consciousness, the hardest and slowest to affect by thought and intention. Accentuating the immediate and ephemeral, the gross man is tossed around by circumstance and has far less willpower or influence than he believes, should he even stop to reflect. He does not appreciate the wider impact of his actions, the karmic consequences, nor realise the cycles and patterns at work in the world.

If talk of consciousness sounds somewhat modern, New Age, or Californian, it is in fact something known to sages of all times. Seventeenth Century master, William Lilly, for example, knew it: 'The holier thou art and the more near God, the purer judgement thou shall give'. He meant that the higher our level of consciousness, the more complete value of an astrological symbol we can realise - except he said it far better. Emphasising the material, Saturnian aspect of the art at the expense of its spiritual soul leads nowhere. Astrologers of all times have always been priests, mystics, hermits and magicians, and the art needs, is not more symbols or technique, but more awareness. Western astrologers seizing upon Jyotish, for example, for its apparently uncompromising determinism, fail to appreciate that symbols manifest in different ways according to the consciousness of the individual. The wise astrologer takes the subject's evolutionary level into account[25].

The divinatory plane that we enter into while studying a horoscope, either on our own or with a client, is a step into spirit. The symbolic planets are there all the time, representing a kind of idealised, higher unified level of creation, which is structured in human consciousness. It is as well, however, not to confuse this divinatory space with the earthier, more mundane 'Saturn level' which most of us live at most of the time. The optimist says we are entirely free, the pessimist that we are completely conditioned, but the Saturn realist knows we transit somewhere between the two. Living according to an idealised picture of the world is perfectly well, but we should not, for example, counsel clients to treat their Income Tax return as pure Mind. Still, astrology counsels optimism: we must believe we can do anything and not be held back. The extent to which we identify with the material Saturnian world is the extent to which we suffer and every effort we make in the direction of Spirit chips away at the prison walls of materialism. There is always something to gain by positive thinking, whereas pessimism leads nowhere.

Admittedly, the fact that Saturn, of all planets, is the ruler of fate has somewhat tyrannical connotations and carries the sense of stoicism in the face of adversity. But the idea of grace or divine intervention can equally easily represent a fated deliverance, when our own efforts and evasions have come to nothing. The law of karma says human life is limited by past deeds, but also by things *not yet done*. This entails a sense of giving expression to a positive destiny, our *dharma*, or cosmic truth. This is worth pointing out, for seemingly inherent in the humanistic outlook is the assumption that fate is a bad thing. It is so often discussed with a sinister subtext, as if love affairs and lottery rollovers are not also gifts from the Gods. Those accepting fate are labelled quiescent and defeatist, and the idea that it is a mystical force to be respected and co-operated with seldom receives much of a hearing. The belief that there are no accidents, and trusting that we are essentially in wiser hands than our lowly perspective permits, is the flip-side of the 'we know everything' view. Serendipity is fate's fortunate face, one of life's rarest pleasures, and not many people would wish to philosophise *it* away.

The *I Ching* also says of this:

> *'Human life on Earth is conditioned and unfree, and when a man recognises this limitation and makes himself dependent upon the harmonious and beneficent forces of the cosmos, he achieves success'.*
> (*Li, The Clinging, Fire*. Wilhelm translation).

For example, Saturn is about to transit a client's natal Tenth house and oppose his natally afflicted Sun, and the hard-line traditional astrologer predicts that his client will get the sack. Weighing up all the planetary strengths and looking at the simultaneous directions for this time, this appears to the astrologer extremely likely, if not inevitable. Forewarned with this prediction, the client is undaunted, and is careful to maintain his performance at the office, arriving extra early, staying late and being extremely nice to everyone. The boss does not like him, he experiences scheming from his co-workers, but he survives the Saturn-Sun transit still holding his job down. Was the traditionalist's prediction wrong? Strictly, perhaps, but it was certainly in the neighbourhood.

There may indeed have been definite attempts to get rid of the man but forewarned and forearmed, he overcame them. It may have been extraordinarily difficult, but he cheated the irrevocable fate predicted, and won the day in the end. Was it worth it? Perhaps after an exhausting experience like this, a more psychologically-oriented astrologer would ask their client to explore the possibility that he is in the wrong job. Or perhaps again, with typical Saturnian irony, the firm goes bankrupt six months later and he is out of work anyway, leaving him wishing that he *had* been fired. Painful and humiliating, no doubt, but equally the kind of wakeup call he needed at the time, giving him a six month head-start towards a new career. Saturn brought its promised sorrow and loss in the immediate term, but it was for a good reason and the client used his experience to plan wisely. It is a matter of perspective.

Strategies for Saturn

So the question remains, what to *do* about a challenging Saturn on the birth-chart? In the practical spirit which has been referred to at points in this book, Saturn likes to act, to make some material change. This is the essential ingredient missing from the clever behavioural insights of Western astrology. So much time is devoted in astrological literature, including this present book, to delineating the exquisite agonies of various planetary influences, which are seen as awesome cosmic obstacles that cannot be overcome, only endured. Counselling may help matters for a while, but we are essentially powerless. In the face of cosmic influences, any practical steps that we attempt seem somewhat vain, shallow or ineffectual: an umbrella in a hurricane.

Astrology is a profound system of knowledge, so highly esoteric that few people, if any, fully understand how it works. Used as a tool for self-awareness is the least that it can do, and far from being a mere intellectual curiosity, knowledge of one's natal chart is its own form of analysis and self-development that is too seldom recognised. A certain amount of space has been given in this discussion to higher consciousness, without pointing out that astrology is itself one of the things that raises our awareness. In the *I Ching*, the diviner is referred to as 'the superior man', and that status may also be applied to the astrologer. Without realising how it happens, astrology is a positive influence that *acts* upon us.

Patience and a positive attitude are common antidotes suggested for Saturn, which at first seems like a cast-iron cop-out, or actually no remedy at all. Rather than a pro-active exploit, thinking positively is seen as somewhat passive: a means of consolation or keeping our spirits up, while patience and serenity are not at much of a premium, either. At a time when we demand miraculous instant fixes for everything, especially the lifestyle accessory of Personal Growth, one cannot for example, imagine a book entitled: *The Patient Approach to Self-Development* making much headway among the best-sellers.

Acceptance and fortitude, however, are valuable attributes in relation to anything like Saturn, which does offer eventual promise. If Saturn were not the planet of maturity, then there would be nothing to be patient *for,* but as we have seen, his best results commonly come after time and experience. The alchemical saying *Festina Lente,* or 'make haste slowly' sums up the proper, deliberate Saturnian attitude. Sometimes there is nothing to be done about his placement and a little acceptance is better than chewing the carpet over things that cannot be changed. Learning to live within our boundaries, not becoming frustrated and above all not comparing ourselves to exaggerated advertising agency notions of what life should be like is something to bear in mind. Allow Saturn some breathing space, don't ignore his prompting and eventually we *do* grow. Saturn's challenge represents a life's experience and if we have to endure frustration and delay in achieving our ends, then the eventual breakthrough is still more gratifying. Satisfaction delayed is satisfaction enhanced.

There are other, more esoteric means, however, which seem to have fallen into disuse and disrepute. Astrological talismans are one means by which we can counteract the effects of the planets, and without which the astrological model is not complete knowledge. Electing a time to construct a talisman is straightforward judicial astrology and can be carried out by anyone with a little knowledge of Elections. Putting the appropriate planet on the ascendant, preferably in aspect to a benefic or well-dignified body, and generally strengthening the significations of the affair we wish to influence. Bringing in herbs, metals and scents to elect the creation of progressively more sophisticated talismans is the next step. Votive offerings to propitiate the planets are a step further still.

Certain gemstones also have a healing or protective effect

over specific planets. This is standard practice in India, part of the essential body of knowledge, where the art and science of astrological gemmology has been established for centuries. Great care is required, however, for it is very easy to strengthen a malefic influence inadvertently. It is also better not to mix and match Tropical astrology with Jyotish, for despite the similarities, the timing and interpretation is quite different. Mantras, or sacred syllables, are also prescribed, which has a kind of counterpart in the Catholic practice of giving Hail Marys and Our Fathers. Mantras fit into the astrological framework of the elements: water purifies earth, fire purifies water, air purifies fire, space purifies air and mantras purify space.

Some practitioners may feel this is too close to overt magic to be entirely comfortable, as if astrology itself is not a magical practice in itself. But this is traditional astrology and a recognition that time itself is a dimension with character and qualities. Others may consider the notion of attempting to circumvent fate in this way simply undignified and that it is better to accept what is coming with philosophic equanimity. Negotiating destiny is spoken of with the same disdain as governments speak of negotiating with terrorists. Yet an astrology that is not problem-solving and pre-emptive is diagnosis without remedy. Along with narrow, ego-oriented, deterministic judgements, this is one of the main reasons for many astrologers' poor, pseudo-mystical reputation[26]. The stoical approach is the default most of us are left with in the absence of viable astrological remedies or palliatives. Lying back and thinking of England is one way, but surely we owe it to ourselves to try something a little more enlightened?

Marsilio Ficino, the renowned renaissance magus had fears,

as to how far the practice of natural magic was contrary to the teachings of the Church. He had something to be worried about. This pious man, who later became an ordained Catholic minister, argued that utilizing astrological correspondences in terms of colour, smell and pictures is not the same as invoking spirits or false idols. There is no use in studying the effects of the stars without exploring and developing the means of counteracting their unwelcome influence. Ficino had a particular interest in finding effective remedies, for he had a quite domineering Saturn in his own chart. In the style of interpretation of his day, he believed that this Saturn would lead to: 'a 'brutish' life, bowed down with the extreme of misery'. Today, we would see this reading not as only harsh, but plain wrong. Should we ever become too nostalgic for the days of strict Saturnian world-view, his words are a useful corrective.

In any event, some of Ficino's suggested remedies for Saturn are not so much different than somebody might get from a conventional doctor if suffering from depression. Ficino recommends that we should take exercise, move about and surround ourselves with the symbolism of the Sun. Saturn is heavy, stuck energy so the counsel to get exercise seems sound. The heat of the Sun infuses a thing with energy, makes it move and become more malleable. It is so easy to get into a negative spiral with hard Saturn transits, when our morale is low and there is a pervasive sense of hopelessness and frustration. It is precisely at these times when we should be most active and alert.

Physical yoga postures are a simpler and possibly even more excellent remedy for heavy Saturn transits; certainly more effective than any purely intellectual therapy. Any state in the mind has a corresponding state in the body and the slow, patient, disciplined approach of yoga is Saturnian in all the best ways. Lethargy and depression are common under difficult Saturn transits and the simplest well-executed asanas bring noticeably increased vitality and happiness. Sometimes a subtle lift such as this is all we need under a heavy dose of Saturn, and it gives us courage to face the future. On a more esoteric level, asanas and their extension of breath control and meditation are ways for the individual to become more inwardly centred and self-referral, rather than Saturnine and object-referral. Yoga makes us look to ourselves for happiness and realisation, rather than being bounced around by the outside world.

Few things show how far the negative Saturnian world-view has permeated than the general contempt in which positive thinking is held. Saturn signifies the immutable, baseline material world and thinking affirmatively is at best a means of keeping one's spirits up, only to experience a yet more bathetic let down when awful reality kicks in. To invoke positive thinking then, as a remedy for objectively difficult factors on the birth chart is to invite ridicule, as in most peoples' eyes positive thinking reads: 'whistling past the graveyard'. Positive thinking is either seen as the complacent psychobabble, or the last recourse of the terminally sad and desperate.

If the key to success were as simple as just thinking positively, then wouldn't we all be world-beaters? Many people see this as the epitome of a bourgeois attitude that does not have much connection with ordinary people's everyday troubles. *But thinking positively is not easy, it is very hard*, especially over a prolonged period. A positive frame of mind is a priceless commodity, however fleeting it may be, while sustained effort in this direction can make an enormous material difference to a life. Something too little mentioned in most New Age literature is that programmed positive thinking also requires patience. Performed with deliberate intent, however, it is simultaneously the subtlest and most powerful process it is possible to enact, and with dense, bottom line reality like Saturn represents, the effects simply take a while to percolate down. Saturn responds magnificently to positive thought backed up with action.

So we need action. For practical purposes, I recommend affirmations: positive, self-confirming statements made in quiet moments or meditation that goes deeper than mere self-analysis. From a karmic perspective, the birth-chart represents the sum of our thoughts and actions, so powerful, purposeful thoughts are like a strong antidote to entrenched patterns that have built up over lifetimes. Thought, especially with positively directed intention is an infinitely powerful material force that overcomes anything, anywhere.

APPENDIX ONE

Astrology down the line

Live telephone readings have become the front-line of astrology. Many astrologers are averse to such overt commercial practices and the typical premium-rate setup may be demeaned as superficial and exploitative, quite removed from the business of a real consultation. Yet callers are frequently taken aback by the depth and detail that can be derived from a chart, and one of the astrologer's main problems is in fact dealing with the client's inflated expectations. Many of them will have seen the telephone number advertised in newspaper or magazine, perhaps next to a Sun-sign column containing a concise general interpretation.

However, any astrologer who has actually worked on commercial phone-lines will confirm that it is quite easy to enter into a strong rapport with clients and it is surprising how much psychic nuance actually comes down the telephone. Dealing with calls from the no-man's land of strangers' real lives, is also a tough assignment and fitting them into an instant astrological framework is a true seasoning process for any aspiring consultant. Given a strict time limit and the fact that people rarely call when their world is spinning around wonderfully, it is as well to get straight to the heart of the matter, which invariably means checking on the position of Saturn. Start by identifying Saturn as the *challenge* at least and use this as the fulcrum of the reading. Even in a full-length hour or ninety minute consultation there is frequently not enough time for the astrologer to showcase their flashy technique, but only to focus on the salient points: the most important planets, the closest natal aspects and the biggest impending transits. A heavily aspected Saturn fulfils all of these criteria.

The Consultation Chart

The inevitability of dirty data in many live astrology situations means that consultation charts come into their own. This is basically a chart for the moment of the phone-call or appointment itself, using not too strict horary rules which seem to reflect the client's overall situation and intentions at the time[27]. It effect, it is very like a Tarot spread. This practice apparently goes against the classical Saturnian model of natal charts based on a fixed moment of origin, and the philosophical implications of such a system are worth investigating - though not here. Suffice it to say astrology is infinitely mysterious and the consultation chart, like horary, operates on a divinatory principle of every instant of time containing the seed of every other: 'To see a world in a grain of sand'. There is a mystical element in the very nature of casting horoscopes that allows us a glimpse into the deeper nature of things.

This is not an argument for the effectiveness of consultation charts over standard natal practice, but they do serve a useful purpose. Many people come to astrologers on the spur of the moment and have one overriding question in mind, as opposed to a desire for lengthy perspectives. The resolution of one issue is what many people expect of an astrology reading, and they are frequently bemused by the request for an accurate birth-time. But at the same time, the horary approach of 'yes or no' answers is an awesome responsibility. Using a consultation chart alongside the natal map places the latter in an immediate context, but unlike horary, there does not need to be a specific question, nor a definite judgement, and the consultation chart does not have to meet exacting standards of radicality.

Still, the basic horary approach can be used, insofar as the client is represented by the ascendant ruler. Frequently, this describes the client's immediate situation and there have been times when this has been all that is required for the reading. It is noticeable that depending on the time of day Saturn may change house three or four times in four hours (the average length of a telephone or exhibition astrologer's shift), and wherever it happens to be in the diurnal cycle is the source of the callers' core problems. So if Saturn starts in the Seventh house of the daily chart, then the callers are in relationship triangles or are contemplating leaving their marriages. Saturn moves backwards into the Sixth house and the calls start to become about the headaches they have been getting from working too much overtime. Then it is the Fifth house and they are getting challenging behaviour from their children; then the Fourth and they want to move home.

Consultation chart example.

My habit had become to see astrology clients at a nearby café, so I would print a chart for the moment of the appointment to take along with me. This did not start out for any express divinatory purpose, but merely so that in the absence of my computer I had the daily planets to refer to in context. It soon occurred to me, however, that there was something more going on:

A young student came for a reading, who was having a complicated time. She had come from the other side of the world to study in London and entered into an affair with one of her male tutors. At the time she came to see me, she had ended the relationship, but still had ties with her tutor, who remained a friend and mentor figure. She had reached the end of her studies and was about to go home for the summer period and break all ties with her ex-lover. She was concerned that he would not be hurt, but her main interest was that her application for a working visa would be successful on

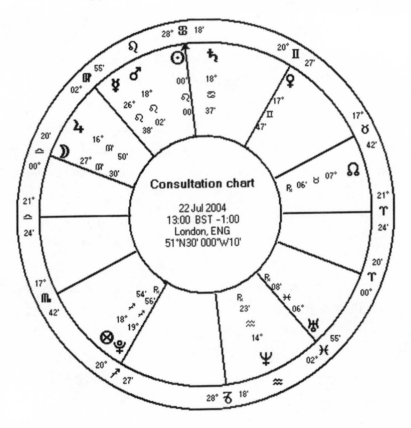

her return to the UK.

Using the chart ruler to represent the client, the chart clearly shows her concerns. Venus is about to enter the Ninth house, which shows her imminent departure for a far away place. It is also about to oppose Pluto, symbolising the final and irrevocable split with her lover. Saturn's placement in the Ninth reveals the worry about her visa application and also the general complication of matters around her studies. This is a very Ninth-house reading, and Saturn's presence here bears out his symbolism as the essential heart of any problem. Find Saturn, find the problem.

From a strict horary point of view, the Moon is void, so the matter would come to nothing. I basically took this to mean she had nothing to worry about, for I sensed from speaking to her that she would make a good case for herself and in crude terms, good immigration material. The Sun at zero degrees Leo on the mid-heaven shows her dignified character and the favourable impression she would make to the authorities. Venus applies by sextile to Mars in the eleventh, so her tutor-lover would still be available as a character witness and support.

I stress that I was not using the consultation chart in any purposely divinatory sense, but simply as background shading to the main business of the natal reading. Any meaning derived from it is purely accidental, but just *look* at it. With the client above, I spend a couple of hours taking her through her natal chart, but I suspect the main thing she took away with her was the positive outlook regarding her visa application. All of this came from the 'day chart'. Repeatedly I have been amazed at the reflections of clients' situations, of which the above example is only one of many. Especially because it is not a horary moment in the strict sense, but simply the most mutually convenient time for the client and I to get together.

APPENDIX 2

ZODIACAL HOUSES.

Houses are a problem in Western astrology – our conventional method of division is not as rigorous or reliable a system as in India, for instance, and it is not straightforward to interpret the intrinsic condition of a house aside from the planets contained within it. There are a score of systems of division, for a start, so the technique of looking at house rulerships, especially of the intermediate cusps, does not provide a very firm base to work with. Some astrologers use Equal house because it is a simple symbolic method, others use Regiomontanus after William Lilly; still others use Koch, partly, one suspects, because it is relatively new. The developments of Project Hindsight have brought to light Whole Sign houses, where the twelve houses run from 0 to 30 degrees of each sign, without regard to the ascendant degree. This, it is claimed, is how the houses were originally intended to work. Vedic astrology, of course, uses this system very effectively, but Jyotish is based on the Sidereal zodiac. The Greeks may have used Whole Sign Houses, and it has the attraction of elegant simplicity, but using it in the Tropical context does not seem to fit.

The examples in this book are erected according to Placidus, despite its well-documented problems; chiefly that it cannot construct horoscopes for extreme Northern latitudes. Opponents of Placidus also point out that it only holds sway because Raphael published tables in his yearly almanac and it became the most readily available and expedient system. But most astrologers use

Placidus for natal work, in preference over the much simpler Equal House for instance, presumably because there is something about it that resonates and has been found to 'work'. This is the 'argument from serendipity'; the fact that it was this system and not some other that Raphael used, and it has stood the test of time.

Index of birth data.

The majority of data comes from Lois Rodden's indispensable **Astro-Data-Bank** software. I have also relied on Frank Clifford's excellent book, *British Entertainers, The Astrological Profiles.* Such large and varied collections of data are all any astrologer needs for new insight and inspiration.

Arnold Schwarzenegger: 30/07/1947, 4:10am MEDT, Graz, Austria, 47N05, 15E27. RR: A

Salman Rushdie:19/06/1947, 2:30am IST, Bombay, India.18N58, 72E50. RR: A

Mick Jagger: 26/07/1943, 2:30am GDWT, Dartford, England, 51N27, 0E17. RR:A

Bill Gates: 28/10/1955, 22:00 PST, Seattle, WA. 47N36, 122W19. RR: A

Sir Richard Branson: 18/07/1950, 7:00am, London, England, 51N00, 0W31, RR: A

Charles Dickens: 07/02/1812, 19:50 LMT, Portsmouth, England,

50N48, 1W05. RR: A

Martin Bashir: 19/01/1963, 12:30 GMT, London UK, 51N30, 0W10. RR: A

Dylan Thomas: 27/10/1914, 20:56 GMT, Swansea, Wales, 51N38, 003W57. RR: C

Jiddu Krishnamurti: 12/05/1895, 00:23 LMT, Mandanapalle, India, 13N33, 78E30. RR: B

Woody Allen: 1/12/1935, 22:55EST, Bronx, NY, 40N51, 73W54. RR: AA

John Lennon: 9/10/1940, 18:30BST, Liverpool, England, 53N25, 002W55. RR: A

Anthony Keidis: 1/11/1962, 5:00am EST, Grand Rapids, MI, 42N57, 085W05

Carl Lewis: 1/07/1961, 07:49 CST, Birmingham AL, 33N31 086W48, RR: A

Eleanor of Aquitaine: 24/09/1122, 15:20 LMT, Chignon, France, 44N50, 000W50. RR: C

Bill Clinton: 19/08/1946, 08:51, Hope, ARK, 33N01, 93W35, RR:A

Elizabeth I: 17/09/1533, 14:54 LMT, London, England. 51N29,

0W0. RR: AA.

Mary Queen of Scots: 18/12/1542, 13:12 LMT, Linlithgow, Scotland. 55N59, 003W37. RR: AA.

Linda McCartney: 24/ 09/1941, 10:00 EDT, New York, NY. 40N42 074W00. RR: A

Sting: 2/10/1951, 01:30 BST, Wallsend, England. 55N00 001W31, RR: A.

George Harrison: 24/02/1943, 23:42 BST, Liverpool, England, 53N25, 002W55. RR: AA

Lee Harvey Oswald: 18/10/1939, 21:55 CST, New Orleans, LA. 29N57 090W04. RR: A

William Lilly: 11/05/1602 NS, 02:00 LMT, Diseworth, England. 52N50, 001W16. RR: A

Muhammad Ali: 17/01/1942, 18:35, Louisville, KY, 38N15, 085W45. RR: AA

Bob Dylan: 24/05/1941, 21:05, Duluth, MN, 46N47, 092W06, RR: AA

Rupert Murdoch: 11/03/1931, 23:59, Melbourne, Australia, 37S49, 144E58. RR: A

Jeffrey Archer: 15/04/1940, 11:45 -1.00, Mark, Somerset, England. 51N00, 002W52. RR: A

Oscar Wilde: 16/10/1854, 3:00 +0:25, Dublin, Eire, 53N20, 006W15. RR: AA

Queen Elizabeth II: 21/04/1926, 02:40 -1:00, London, England, 51N30 000W10. RR: AA

Bob Geldof: 5/10/1951, 14:20 BST, Dublin, Eire, 53N20, 006W15. RR: A

Martin Luther King: 15/01/1929, 12:00 CST, Atlanta, GA, 33N44, 084W23. RR: A

Paul McCartney: 18/06/1942, 14:00 -2:00, Liverpool, England, 53N25, 002W55. RR: A

Alan Leo: 07/08/1860 NS, 05:49 GMT, London, England, 51N30, 000W09, RR: B

Frank Sinatra: 12/12/1915, 3:00 EST, Hoboken, NJ, 40N44, 074W02. RR:A

NOTES

1 Uranus also represents the flash of intuitive insight that is part of every astrologer's experience.

2 Try reconciling it to yourself, for that matter.

3 See Robert Hand, *Horoscope Symbols* – A short, but brilliant exposition of the core meaning of Saturn, which he links to the attributes of the 90° square aspect.

4 The progressed Moon's 28 year orbit reflects Saturn's transits very well.

5 If there is any value in the terms 'benefic' and 'malefic', I suggest *benefic* is planetary energy which allows us to *be*, while malefic is the same which requires us to *become*, in the sense of making an adjustment.

6 Neptune is clearly another a very *weird* planet, in the sense of mysticism or enchantment. Saturn's weirdness, however, is specifically to do with fate.

7 Bible, Proverbs. 23:7

8 Punk rock first appeared in 1976-77, while Saturn transited Leo.

9 In fact, the natal house of Venus shows where we can find glamour, escapism and fun outside of the usual source, relationships.

10 Vedic authorities for instance state that an ideal human life should encompass all of the *dasas*, or planetary periods; a span of one hundred and twenty years, or *four* Saturn returns. Perhaps the reason the initial Saturn return is commonly found to be quite overwhelming is that it is intended as only the first quarter of a four-fold experience.

11 Stephen Arroyo, *Astrology, Karma and Transformation*

12 A perfect example of Saturn at work is with Neptune's
    original discovery. Neptune had been spotted in the sky at
    intervals since the time of Galileo, but was only definitively
    identified as a planet in on 23rd September 1846, while
    closely conjunct Saturn.

13 The definitive experience of Saturn transiting a natal house is
    a good technique to use for chart rectification. Reverse
    engineering a birth time is a notoriously difficult business,
    but finding out the client's main source of difficulty at any
    given time is a useful and sometimes quite immediate way of
    sketching the layout of a chart.

14 See Appendix 1. The Zodiacal Houses.

15 Liz Greene's *Relating* is an excellent book on this subject,
    from where I have taken the phrase 'Inner Partner'.

16 In the light of Ali's natal Mars in the Ninth house, The
    Vietnam War must have appeared a kind of misguided
    political *jihad*

17 Erin Sullivan, *Saturn in Transit*

18 Anyone practicing fortune telling was defined as a 'scoundrel
    and vagabond' and repeat offences made them 'an
    incorrigible vagabond'(!) (My thanks to astrologer Jane
    Amanda for this note)

19 Composite charts are often very revealing, especially the
    conjunctions, if conventional synastry does not point up
    obvious connections between two people.

20 Liz Greene in *A New Look At An Old Devil* also points out
    the significance of orbs in Saturn synastry and suggests that
    three degrees or less becomes difficult.

21 This may be extended to Saturn-Sun and Saturn-Moon contacts, too.

22 Indeed technically *illegal* until as recently as the 1980s.

23 See Geoffrey Cornelius's *The Moment of Astrology*: an eloquent and closely-argued presentation of the case for astrology as divination. Significantly, Cornelius equates the intuitive faculty of astrologers with what he terms 'Psi-Neptune', with Neptune representing the boundless in astrology as opposed to the limitations of Saturn.

24 Craft quirks such as getting unexpected insights from 'wrong charts' have not only survived into the computer age, they seem often to have escalated Computers do not have native symbolic sense and pressing the wrong key can produce errors quite beyond the scope of mistaken calculation by hand.

25 This cannot necessarily be determined from the chart per se, but intuitively, from the extent to which the client has a spiritual or holistic perspective.

26 Astrology is seen as a sentimental world view, a parlour game without any real power to influence the outcome of what it predicts, even if its predictions are correct.

27 Adrian Duncan's *Doing Time on Planet Earth* and Wanda Sellar's *The Consultation Chart* are two dedicated textbooks on this technique.

O

is a symbol of the world,
of oneness and unity. O Books
explores the many paths of wholeness
and spiritual understanding which
different traditions have developed down
the ages. It aims to bring this knowledge
in accessible form, to a general readership,
providing practical spirituality to today's seekers.

For the full list of over 200 titles covering:

- CHILDREN'S PRAYER, NOVELTY AND GIFT BOOKS
- CHILDREN'S CHRISTIAN AND SPIRITUALITY
- CHRISTMAS AND EASTER
- RELIGION/PHILOSOPHY
- SCHOOL TITLES
- ANGELS/CHANNELLING
- HEALING/MEDITATION
- SELF-HELP/RELATIONSHIPS
- ASTROLOGY/NUMEROLOGY
- SPIRITUAL ENQUIRY
- CHRISTIANITY, EVANGELICAL
AND LIBERAL/RADICAL
- CURRENT AFFAIRS
- HISTORY/BIOGRAPHY
- INSPIRATIONAL/DEVOTIONAL
- WORLD RELIGIONS/INTERFAITH
- BIOGRAPHY AND FICTION
- BIBLE AND REFERENCE
- SCIENCE/PSYCHOLOGY

Please visit our website,
www.O-books.net

SOME RECENT O BOOKS

The Instant Astrologer
A revolutionary new book and software package for the astrological seeker
Lyn Birkbeck
2nd printing
The brilliant Lyn Birkbeck's new book and CD package, The Instant Astrologer, combines modern technology and the wisdom of the ancients, creating an invitation to enlightenment for the masses, just when we need it most!
Astrologer **Jenny Lynch**, Host of NYC's StarPower Astrology Television Show
1903816491 628pp full colour throughout with CD ROM 240/180
£39 $69 cl

Astro-Wisdom
The knowledge, love and power in your stars
Lyn Birkbeck
This goes beyond the populist territory of Sun Sign astrology. The author explains the impact of planetary cycles on our lives...In the final chapter, Birkbeck offers further useful insights into the qualities associated with the sun, moon and planets and their meaning in our own birth charts. Astro-Wisdom is accessible for those with little or no knowledge of astrology as an introductory and practical astrology book. **Light**
1903816564 288pp **£9.99 $14.95**

Divine Astrology: Cosmic Reconnection

Lyn Birkbeck

An inspirational, evolutionary approach to astrology daring us to link to the Divine. **Richard Beaumont**, Kindred Spirit

1905047037 228pp+40 colour cards in boxed set **£17.99 $29.95**

Let the Numbers Guide You
The spiritual science of numerology

Shiv Sharan Singh

2nd printing

Like no other teacher, he has simplified and de-mystified the logic inherent in mathematical truths. Discarding the convoluted occult schools of numerology, he brings forth simple truths which are accessible to everyone.

Alma Fahre Mecattaf, Consultant and Yoga Teacher

1903816645 320pp **£11.99 $17.95**

Let the Stars Illuminate Your Career Path

Mwezi Mtoto

With the information in this book you will be able to choose the work you love, and love the work you choose.

1846940214 128pp **£9.99 $14.95**

Past Lives Astrology
Understanding reincarnation through your astrological chart

Adam Fronteras

This book explores how karma and astrology work, the theories and beliefs. Using your date of birth and the astrological positions of the planets and in particular the retrograde planets we can find out who and when you lived. All tables are included and can be used by non-astrologers to gain insight into the lessons of the past and the lessons that you are here to learn now.

1846940222 226pp **£11.99 $21.95**

Tarot for the Curious Spirit

Barbara Venn-Lever

A descriptive guide written in an easy-to-read format that will make discovering, exploring and learning about the tarot interesting and informative. An absolute font of wisdom, and a lucid communicator.
Dr Keith Hearne, Principal of the European College of Hypnotherapy.

1846940036 260pp £11.99 $19.95

When Stars Collide
Why we love who we love and when we love them

Paul Westran

A superb book on how relationships can be analyzed moving through time. His marriage of progression and synastry technique being used to illustrate when lovers meet, how they grow and evolve together, and why they arrive at points of conflict over time, will raise astrological relationship analysis to a more sophisticated level.
Robert P. Blaschke, author of the *Astrology: A Language of Life* series.

1905047746 360pp **£16.99 $29.95**

The 7 Ahas! of Highly Enlightened Souls
How to free yourself from ALL forms of stress
Mike George
7th printing
A very profound, self empowering book. Each page bursting with wisdom and insight. One you will need to read and reread over and over again! **Paradigm Shift**
1903816319 128pp 190/135mm **£5.99 $11.95**

God Calling
A Devotional Diary
A. J. Russell
46th printing
Perhaps the best-selling devotional book of all time, over 6 million copies sold.
1905047428 280pp 135/95mm **£7.99** cl.
US rights sold

The Goddess, the Grail and the Lodge
The Da Vinci code and the real origins of religion
Alan Butler
5th printing
This book rings through with the integrity of sharing time-honoured revelations. As a historical detective, following a golden thread from the great Megalithic cultures, Alan Butler vividly presents a compelling picture of the fight for life of a great secret and one that we simply can't afford to ignore. From the foreword by **Lynn Picknett & Clive Prince**
1903816696 360pp 230/152mm **£12.99 $19.95**

The Heart of Tantric Sex

A sourcebook on the practice of Tantric sex

Diana Richardson

3rd printing

One of the most revolutionary books on sexuality ever written.
Ruth Ostrow, News Ltd.

1903816378 256pp **£9.99 $14.95**

I Am With You

The best-selling modern inspirational classic

John Woolley

14th printing hardback

Probably the consistently best-selling devotional in the UK today.

0853053413 280pp 150x100mm **£9.99** cl

4th printing paperback

1903816998 280pp 150/100mm **£6.99 $12.95**

In the Light of Meditation

The art and practice of meditation in 10 lessons

Mike George

2nd printing

A classy book. A gentle yet satisfying pace and is beautifully illustrated. Complete with a CD or guided meditation commentaries, this is a true gem among meditation guides. **Brainwave**

1903816610 224pp 235/165mm full colour throughout +CD **£11.99 $19.95**

Is There An Afterlife?
A comprehensive overview of the evidence, from east and west
David Fontana
2nd printing
An extensive, authoritative and detailed survey of the best of the evidence supporting survival after death. It will surely become a classic not only of parapsychology literature in general but also of survival literature in particular. Professor Fontana is to be congratulated on this landmark study and I thoroughly recommend it to all who are really interested in a serious exploration of the subject. **Universalist**
1903816904 496pp 230/153mm **£14.99 $24.95**

The Reiki Sourcebook
Bronwen and Frans Stiene
5th printing
It captures everything a Reiki practitioner will ever need to know about the ancient art. This book is hailed by most Reiki professionals as the best guide to Reiki. For an average reader, it's also highly enjoyable and a good way to learn to understand Buddhism, therapy and healing. **Michelle Bakar**, Beauty magazine
1903816556 384pp **£12.99 $19.95**

Soul Power
The transformation that happens when you know
Nikki de Carteret
4th printing
This may be one of the finest books in its genre today. Using scenes from her own life and growth, Nikki de Carteret weaves wisdom

about soul growth and the power of love and transcendent wisdom gleaned from the writings of the mystics. This is a book that I will read gain and again as a reference for my own soul growth. She is a scholar who is totally accessible and grounded in the human experience. **Barnes and Noble review**
190381636X 240pp **£9.99 $15.95**

Colours of the Soul
Transform your life through colour therapy
June McLeod
A great book, the best I've read on the subject and so inspirational.
Laura, Helios Centre
1905047258 176pp + 4pp colour insert **£11.99 $21.95**

Crystal Prescriptions
The A-Z guide to over 1,200 symptoms and their healing crystals
Judy Hall
2nd printing
Another potential best-seller from Judy Hall. This handy little book is packed as tight as a pill-bottle with crystal remedies for ailments. It is written in an easy-to-understand style, so if you are not a virtuoso with your Vanadinite, it will guide you. If you love crystals and want to make the best use of them, it is worth investing in this book as a complete reference to their healing qualities. **Vision**
1905047401 176pp 2 colour **£7.99 $15.95**

Grow Youthful

David Niven Miller

A practical, extensive guide covering everything you can do to avoid ageing.

1846940044 224pp **£10.00 $19.95**

The Healing Power of Celtic Plants

Healing herbs of the ancient Celts and their Druid medicine men

Angela Paine

Each plant is covered here in depth, explaining its history, myth and symbolism and also how to grow, preserve, prepare and use them. Uniquely, here, their properties are examined together with the scientific evidence that they work.

1905047622 240pp 250/153mm b/w illustrations **£16.99 $29.95**

The Healing Sourcebook

Learn to heal yourself and others

David Vennells

Here is the distilled wisdom of many years practice; a number of complementary therapies which are safe, easy to learn from a book, and combine wonderfully with each other to form a simple but powerful system of healing for body and mind.

1846940052 320pp **£14.99 $22.95**

Healing the Eternal Soul

Insights from past life and spiritual regression

Andy Tomlinson

Written with simple precision and sprinkled with ample case examples this will be an invaluable resource for those who assist others in achieving contact with the eternal part of themselves. It is an invaluable contribution and advancement to the field of Regression Therapy. More so, it is an incredibly interesting read! **Dr. Arthur E. Roffey**, Past Vice-President, Society for Spiritual Regression

190504741X 288pp **£14.99 $29.95**

Humming Your Way to Happiness
An introduction to Tuva and overtone singing from around the world

Peter Galgut

An engaging tour of the field by a medical scientist that takes the reader into the cross-cultural landscape of sound, with special emphasis on Tuva and overtone singing. The author puts his journey into a wide context so that the reader can understand the role that sounds have played in various parts of the world, and also considers sounds, music and religions as well as the use of sound therapy. **Scientific and Medical Network Review**

1905047142 144pp **£9.99 $19.95**

The Invisible Disease
The dangers of environmental illnesses caused by electromagnetic fields and chemical emissions

Gunni Nordstrom

Highly recommended. This most informative and well written book makes the connections between the ranges of illnesses and chemicals used in the manufacture of modern appliances that are mistakenly considered safe. They are not. **Luminous Times**

1903816718 256pp £9.99 **$14.95**

Masters of Health

The original sources of today's alternative therapies

Robert van de Weyer

Here are the major original texts, from eastern and western traditions, rendered into modern idiom. With introductions to each, they form a summary of ancient wisdom on human wholeness.

1905047150 192pp **£9.99 $19.95**

The Theorem

A complete answer to human behaviour

Douglas Arone

Arguably the genius of any great discovery lies in its originality- a fresh idea that is set to challenge traditional modes of thinking while advancing man's march along the path of progress. Far from the idea that the human foetus is cocooned from the cares and woes of existence, our first experience of fear, joy and sorrow actually precedes our birth. This in a nutshell is what this book is set to tell the world. (The author) has accomplished his task with exceptional brilliance. **B. K. Abolade MD**; MRCP (UK), Child and Adolescent Psychiatrist, Alabama

190504710X 496pp **£19.99 $39.95**

Universal Principles and the Metamorphic Technique

The keys to healing and enlightenment

Gaston St-Pierre

It has slowly and quietly gained respect from not only those whose lives have been transformed by it, but from doctors and specialists impressed with the results for conditions ranging from doctors and specialists impressed with the results for conditions ranging from

dyslexia to eating disorders. **Lorna V.** *The Sunday Times*
1903816610 308pp **£11.99 $19.95**

A-Z of Reiki Pocketbook
Everything About Reiki
Bronwen and Frans Stiene
A-Z of Reiki, the latest work by Bronwen and Frans Stiene, is an all-encompassing and expansive glossary of Reiki and Japanese healing. This book helps clear the way for everyone to partake of Reiki. **Nina Paul**, author of *Reiki for Dummies*
1905047894 272pp 125/90mm **£7.99 $16.95**

Energy Works!
Initiation without a master
Teresa Parrott and Graham Crook
Graham and Teresa have explored the world of SKHM to a depth that few have been able to achieve, and, most importantly, they have been able to share their experience with others through their words in the most beautiful way. Those who read about their experience will be initiated in a journey of the heart. I highly recommend allowing yourself to experience that journey. **Patrick Zeigler**
1905047525 304pp **£12.99 $24.95**

Healing Hands
Simple and practical reflexology techniques for developing god health and inner peace
David Vennells
Promising good health and inner peace, this practical guide to reflexology techniques may not be a glossy affair but it is

thoroughly and clearly illustrated. Hand reflexology isn't as well known as the foot variety, but it's undeniably effective and, perhaps most usefully, it's a technique that can be applied for self-treatment. Whatever the healing process is that you're going through, whenever you're experiencing it, Healing Hands can support your journey. **Wave**
1905047126 192pp **£9.99 $16.95**

The Japanese Art of Reiki
A practical guide to self healing
Bronwen and Frans Stiene
2nd printing
This is a sequel to the aclaimed "Reiki Sourcebook." For those of us in the West who see adverts for weekend Reiki Master courses and wonder about the authenticity of the tradition, this book is an eye-opener. It takes the reader back to the Japanese roots of the tradition in a way that conveys its inspirational power and cultural flavour. The book is illustrated and is full of practical guidance for both practitioners and general readers. **Scientific and Medical Network Review**
1905047029 208pp **£12.99 $19.95**

The Creative Christian
God and us; Partners in Creation
Adrian B. Smith
Enlivening and stimulating, the author presents a new approach to Jesus and the Kingdom he spoke of, in the context of the evolution of our Universe. He reveals its meaning for us of the 21st century.
Hans Schrenk, Lecturer in Holy Scripture and Biblical Languages,

Middlesex University.
1905047754 160pp **£11.99 $24.95**

The Gospel of Falling Down

Mark Townsend

This little book is tackling one of the biggest and deepest questions which, unexpectedly, brings us to the foundation of the Christian faith. Mark has discovered this through his own experience of falling down, or failure. **Bishop Stephen Verney**

1846940095 144pp **£9.99 $16.95**

I Still Haven't Found What I'm Looking For

Paul Walker

Traditional understandings of Christianity may not be credible perhaps they can still speak to us in a different way. Perhaps they point to something which we can still sense. Something we need in our lives. Something not just to make us decent, or responsible, but happy and fulfilled. Paul Walker, former *Times* preacher of the year, does not give answers, but rejoices in the search.

1905047762 144pp **£9.99 $16.95**